THE AUDITION BIBLE should be the canon to any actor looking to understand the business. Holly uses her award-winning talent to meticulously dive into the world of casting and share her knowledge. Having worked with Holly on a number of hit television shows, I have seen firsthand her masterful approach to casting … this book contains all the elements to prepare an actor for success.

– **David Janollari**, Executive Producer
David Janollari Entertainment
Six Feet Under, One on One, The Hughleys
PGA Award winner / Emmy Nominee

Good for you for inspiring so many to do better, be better … and hopefully look at auditions as an opportunity to ACT because that's what they are!

– **Dan Bucatinsky**, Actor/Writer/Producer
Scandal, Grey's Anatomy, The Comeback
Emmy Award winner

Actors who have read Holly's book are easy to spot. Their auditions are prepared, passionate, and compelling. They honor the material and make it sing by making it personal. This makes THE AUDITION BIBLE a gift, not only to actors, but also to the writers and directors who work with them.

– **Scott Williams**, Writer/Executive Producer
NCIS, Castle, Bones

What impressed me most about THE AUDITION BIBLE is that it has relevance to anyone who works in front of or behind the camera. It's not just for actors.

– **Noel Clarke**, Actor/Writer/Producer/Director
Star Trek Into Darkness, Kidulthood, Doctor Who
BAFTA & Olivier Award winner

Holly Powell has written a most thorough book on auditioning that I wish I'd had when I was starting out. Holly's wisdom will save every serious actress and actor loads of time and heartache ~ read it now!

– **Frances Fisher**, Actress
Resurrection, Titanic

Holly Powell has crafted an invaluable tool for the young performer as well as seasoned working actor. THE AUDITION BIBLE takes the "SCARY" out of the audition process. Her insight and knowledge of the "business of show" should be the go to source in every performer's arsenal … I haven't come across anything to compare it to.

– **James Pickens, Jr.**, Actor
Grey's Anatomy, 42, The X-Files
NAACP Image Awards winner / SAG Awards winner

Holly brings her considerable experience working with and observing actors and shares a wealth of information to help anyone working in the business of entertainment, be it as an actor, casting director, agent, manager, director or producer.

– **Jason La Padura**, Casting Director
Teen Beach Movie, High School Musical, Heroes, Longtime Companion
CSA Artios Award / Emmy Nominee

I have seen first-hand the professionalism and grace of Ms. Powell in action … This is the clearest, most helpful Bible for the real world of auditioning I have ever read ... The actor as athlete thread is inspiring … It's a must for actors. Bravo! Out of the park!

– **Sam Anderson**, Actor/Director
Justified, Lost, ER

Using her vast and rich experience as a teacher and award-winning casting director, Holly answers questions a young actor might not even have thought of. She knows the terrors an actor can face as he begins the journey and calmly and comfortingly reassures as she provides a sensible road map.

– **Reed Birney**, Actor
House of Cards, Casa Valentina, Circle Mirror Transformation
Drama Desk & Obie Award winner / Tony Award Nominee

Walking in the audition room is the job! Being on set or stage is the Dream. THE AUDITION BIBLE helps one's preparation and confidence in making your dreams come true!

– **Andre Royo**, Actor
The Wire, Fringe

Holly is a caring skilled guide to the whole artistic process of presenting your acting skills in the best form so you can win roles. I worked with Holly when casting my own material and … THE AUDITION BIBLE is the real thing: Easy to read, caring, and effective!

– **Pen Densham**, Producer/Writer/Director
Moll Flanders, Robin Hood: Prince of Thieves, The Outer Limits
CableACE Award winner / Oscar Nominee

Holly Powell shares her years of casting expertise in this smart, practical how-to bible. If you want to book jobs, read it!

– **Mary Lou Belli**, Director/Author
The NEW Sitcom Career Book, Directors Tell The Story
Emmy Award winner

THE AUDITION BIBLE

Secrets Every Actor Needs To Know

Holly Powell

THE AUDITION BIBLE
Secrets Every Actor Needs To Know

Holly Powell

Published in Los Angeles in 2014 by

TAVIN PRESS
2418 N. Keystone St.
Burbank, CA 91504

ISBN 0-9772911-6-2
ISBN13 978-0-9772911-6-8

Library of Congress Control Number: 2014942936

This book was Designed and Produced by TAVIN PRESS
Printed by McNaughton & Gunn, Saline, Michigan
Manufactured in the United States of America

Edited by Paul J. Salamoff

Front Cover Photo by Susan Sheridan Photography

Back Cover Photo by Kelsey Edwards Photography

To my boys,
Christopher & Ryan Wright,
whose unconditional love is everything

Contents

PART ONE
The Audition

ACKNOWLEDGMENTS

My deep love and appreciation to Minda Burr and the Monday Night Master Mind Writing Group: Todd Robert Anderson, Savannah Boucher, Catherine Curry-Williams, Suze Lanier-Bramlett, Tamara Mark, Hilarie Thompson Ormsby, Jonny Solomon, Ramey Warren, and Jennifer White. Without your inspiration, notes, and feedback, this book may never have seen the light of day.

I am fortunate to have had angels appear in this process. Pen Densham, for whom I cast *The Twilight Zone, Carrie,* and *Magnificent 7,* tops the list, for his encouragement and support. Pen led me to Paul J. Salamoff, my editor, whose enthusiasm, wisdom, and creative wizardry propelled this book into creation.

Kate Zentall tweaked and polished, using her magic touch with her copyediting skills. Monica Faulkner supplied her eagle-eyed proofreading. Milo Gould created the original artwork for the book cover. Susan Sheridan brought the cover to life through her gift of photography. Leslie McManus, my website and SEO guru, single-handedly brought me screaming into the Internet age. Mary Lou Belli, Kimberly Jentzen, Diane Christiansen, and Susan Zachary were always there for me with their expert advice. Cathey Painter and Debbie Noodleman were my cheerleaders, and Corabel Shofner, my childhood friend, helped with the very first draft when it was just an idea in my head.

I am also grateful to my sisters, Janis Powell and Nancy Powell Bartlett, teachers, speakers, and business owners in their own right, for not only guiding me with their expertise but inspiring me and cultivating my imagination when we were kids, playing the piano and creating magical characters ... even if I did always have to play the bad fairy.

To my mother, Mavis, who always encouraged me to get out into the world and be the best I could be. And to my father, Joe, who is on the other side marveling how his love of the theater and show business continues to inspire me to this day.

And of course, thanks to all the thousands of actors who helped morph my audition workshops in directions I never could have imagined. As the workshop grew, this book crystallized its focus, and each of you have been inspirational in creating it.

INTRODUCTION

I came up with the idea and format of my audition workshops while I was still casting. I had seen the casting world over a period of twenty-three years from three different points of view: as an independent casting director, as a Network Casting Executive at CBS, and as Senior Vice President of Talent and Casting for The Greenblatt Janollari Studio, Bob Greenblatt and David Janollari.

As I sat in all those audition rooms over the years, I observed the various ways actors dealt with repeated auditions. I noticed the differences in how they walked into the audition room, how they handled pressure as the job got closer, and how they grappled with testing at the network. Some were much more successful than others, and the actors who penetrated the mystique of the audition process were usually the ones who booked the part. And I have to tell you, the part didn't always go to the most talented actor.

When actors train in acting schools, college theater programs, or with acting coaches, they are honing their craft and practicing the art of "being." They follow teachers who preach their belief in the Method, the Meisner Technique, or a hybrid that has morphed into their own technique. Training as an actor is imperative. Scene-study classes, improv classes, comedy classes, commercial classes, voice classes are all necessary so an actor will be prepared when cast and working with other professional actors on a film set, a television show, or a stage play.

But a big reality check can come due when actors finish all their training and are ready to begin the audition process. Most acting classes and schools don't cover the very important skill of auditioning. Actors can experience a deep disconnect between all the amazing training they have had and the sabotaging effects of the audition room. Conquering the audition process and mastering the necessary tools to book the part is a skill each actor must perfect to survive as a professional.

In my audition workshops at Holly Powell Studios, my mission is to demystify the audition process for actors and guide them into adopting the mental focus of an athlete. Through my **6 AUDITION TOOLS METHOD**, actors learn to control sabotaging thoughts by focusing on simple tasks and tapping into and creating specific visualizations, and in the process they obtain complete confidence and presence in the moment.

I send out audition scenes the day before we start the first class and ask actors to prepare the scenes as if they have a real audition. This includes coming dressed the way they would for this audition. The actors have already emailed me their picture and resume, and I choose their scenes based on these two most important actor tools. They don't know it yet, but submitting their picture and resume to me is their first class lesson. *Do they actually look like their headshot? Is their resume in a professional format?*

During class, I then read with each actor as the casting director, while other actors sit in and act as the producers and the director to simulate the real audition room. This allows actors to experience both sides of casting. All the auditions are on-camera and recorded for future viewing.

THE AUDITION BIBLE: **Secrets Every Actor Needs to Know** was written as a companion piece to my audition workshops. It covers not only audition techniques and tools but answers many common questions about audition protocol. Anecdotal audition stories exemplify what works and what doesn't during the casting process.

I mainly cast for television during my career and that is my expertise, but over the years I've also cast theater, film, and commercials. Even though the format of this book often hews to television, an audition is an audition is an audition. All the tools and rules apply for any type of casting session.

PART 1: THE AUDITION is a handbook for any actor auditioning for any venue, be it television, film, theater, a commercial, or a webisode. We follow the actor as he travels through waiting in the lobby, walking into the audition room, the audition itself, the people he encounters in the room, and finally exiting the audition room.

PART 2: AUDITIONING FOR A SERIES-REGULAR ROLE follows the "Pre-Read-To-Network" format that I teach in my audition workshops (or as some managers and agents have started calling it, "The Pilot Class"). The actor is guided through the four steps it typically takes to book a series-regular role on a network television series:

1. The Pre-Read with the Casting Director
2. The Callback for Producers
3. Reading for Studio Executives
4. Testing at the Network

Even though the format in **PART 2** is specifically geared toward auditioning for television, all actors in every medium will find invaluable information that will apply to their individual audition circumstances.

Last, I want to say that this book was not necessarily written to be read from cover to cover. I envision readers combing the table of contents and discovering the exact answer they need for their audition in half an hour: *Should I use props in the audition? What should I wear? Do I need to memorize the material?*

Over my many years as a casting director, I've auditioned more actors than I could possibly count or remember, but what I do remember is watching some very special actors walk through the door during their early years of auditioning: Hilary Swank, Sharon Stone, Reese Witherspoon, George Clooney, Ryan Reynolds, Leonardo DiCaprio, Brad Pitt, Naomi Watts, Patricia Clarkson, Mercedes Ruehl, Stephen Dorff, and Melissa Leo as well as many other talented professionals who went on to establish very successful careers as working actors. What I remember most is *how* these actors walked into the audition room ... with laser focus and confidence.

As I shifted my attention from casting to teaching, it was a natural progression to morph these two worlds during the formation of my audition workshops. I had the good fortune to witness the audition process from three vantage points: as an independent, studio, and network casting director.

Because of this unique perspective, my audition workshops allow actors at any stage of their career to exercise their audition muscle, rediscover the excitement of the process, and hone newly formed skills to tackle and conquer the audition.

It's my sincere hope that this book and these tools will demystify the audition process and help you walk into your auditions fully prepared, confident, with complete presence in the moment, and comfortable in your own skin.

Happy auditioning!

Holly Powell
Los Angeles, California
October 2014

PART ONE

THE AUDITION

au•di•tion [aw-**dish**-*uh* n]

noun

1. a test at which a performer or musician is asked to demonstrate his ability for a particular role
2. a short performance that an actor, musician, dancer, etc. gives in order to show they are suitable for a particular play, film, show
3. something that is heard

verb

1. to judge by means of or be tested in an audition
2. to take part in a trial performance
3. to give a short performance in order to show that you are suitable for a part in a film, play, show, etc., or to make someone do this

word origin

From Latin *auditio* a hearing, from audire to hear. First known use: 1599, *"power of hearing"* Middle French *audicion*

synonyms

test, screen test

CHAPTER 1

BEFORE YOUR AUDITION

* * * * * * * * * * * * * * * *

Never give up on what you really want to do. The person with big dreams is more powerful than the one with all the facts.

Albert Einstein

1.1 EDUCATE YOURSELF

Thinking back over the thousands of actors who stood in front of me before they began their audition, the ones who made the greatest first impressions were the ones who walked in and said, "Hi, Holly!" I know that seems obvious and simplistic, but more times than not actors would walk into the audition room looking like a deer in the headlights. The mere fact that they barely mumbled hi would tip me off that they probably didn't have a clue who I was. Worse would be when they would say, "Nice to meet you," even though I had auditioned them many times before.

Casting directors are people too, and it goes a long way when you call them by name and have educated yourself as to what they have previously cast. Genuine human-to-human contact, knowing the name of the person you are auditioning for, helps defuse the discomfort of that moment, even when the casting director is in a less than stellar mood. I still get surprised today when I am talking to an actor about an audition he went in on and he doesn't remember who the casting director was.

Before an audition, an actor almost always will get a breakdown of the script that lists all the characters and a synopsis of the story. The breakdown also lists the executive producers, writers, director, casting director, studio, and network. It is the actor's job to know just who'll be running the audition and who's likely to be there.

Today, in the wonderful world of IMDb (Internet Movie Database), all this information is at your fingertips. If you've never met this casting director before, type her name into IMDb and check out her previous credits. I was always impressed when an actor would comment on something I had cast, because it showed they'd done their homework on me.

Several years back, I was casting the wonderful pilot *Beck and Call*, written by the multi-talented Dan Bucatinsky (*Scandal*). His producing partner was Lisa Kudrow (*Friends*), and both Dan's and Lisa's names were listed on the breakdown under executive producers. Dan and Lisa were, of course, in every producers' casting session. The first week of casting I became a little unnerved at how one professional actor after another walked into the audition room and upon seeing Lisa Kudrow front row and center had a little freak-out or gush session. "Oh wow, I love your work!" "Oh wow, I didn't know that you would actually be in the room!" "Oh wow, now I'm nervous! I'm such a fan!" And this from actors with long resumes. Really?

An actress I talked to in the lobby said she hadn't known that Lisa would be in the room and her presence really threw her. I said, "Didn't you look at the breakdown? Her name is listed as executive producer." "Well, I did, but I didn't think she'd actually *be* here!" Ultimately, we put a baseball cap on Lisa and sat her toward the back of the room.

Of course I understand that it's only human to get a little star-struck and tongue-tied around someone famous who you admire. However, a professional actor must acknowledge that this is his chosen career and he belongs in this heady company. So if Steven Spielberg's name is listed as executive producer on the breakdown, prepare yourself that he might actually be in the room.

It is also imperative that the actor knows the *tone* of the script. If the audition is for television, then find out what network it is or will be on. A series on CBS is very different in tone from a series on the Disney Channel. If the audition is for an episodic show currently on television, absolutely watch an episode of the series to figure out the tone of the show. Actors today have the advantage of Hulu and other sites to watch on-demand television. There's no excuse to have never seen an episode of the show being auditioned for and then claim confusion about the tone. Again, do your homework.

Is the script a comedy, drama, or dramedy? One of my students told me he'd had an audition for the pilot of *Desperate Housewives*. On the breakdown it said "One-Hour Pilot, ABC." Assuming that all one-hour pilots were dramas, he took this information into the audition room and read the scene as a straight drama with no humor at all. It was the worst audition he ever had. Knowing what we all know now about *Desperate Housewives* (it was a one-hour dramedy with lots of tongue-in-cheek humor), the mental image of this actor's audition is truly painful. I told him afterward if he had IMDb'd Marc Cherry, the creator and writer of the show, he would have seen that Marc had previously written mainly comedies—*The Golden Girls*, *The Crew*, and *The 5 Mrs. Buchanans*. That would have at the very least given him a tip-off on the intended tone of this new pilot. Of course this isn't always the case, as sometimes creators try new genres, but at least the actor would have taken a reasonable approach to the material based on the creator's past credits, instead of making an uninformed assumption.

* * * * * * * * * * * * * * * *

Hilary Swank walked into the audition room and said, "Hi, Holly, nice to meet you." She had done her homework. Not only had she completely educated herself as to who all the players were in the producing of this pilot, she knew the name of the casting director she was going in to meet. She was extremely present and single-mindedly focused. Here was an actress who truly understood the casting director's role of gatekeeper.

As a casting director, wouldn't I be more predisposed to champion and root for an actor who had educated herself as to who I was in the food chain over an actor I'd read ten times before and who still didn't have a clue who I was? It's only human.

* * * * * * * * * * * * * * * *

Use all the resources available to you so you never walk into an audition room again without being completely educated as to who, what, when, and where.

1.2 Memorization

One of the first questions actors ask in my audition workshops is, “Should I memorize the material?” Most people would tell you, “Yes, absolutely.” My take on it is a little different after watching thousands of auditions over the years.

If you have an audition with the casting director and you’ve gotten the material the day before or last minute, the most important thing you can do is make sure you understand the material completely. *Where does the scene take place? Who are you talking to, and how do you feel about that person? What do you want? What happened right before the scene starts?* When actors first get the sides, the temptation is to look at them fast and count their lines. This is one of the worst things you can do. Sit down and read the scene silently to yourself, including all the stage directions, making sure you grasp all that the writer has intended. If there are crossed-out sections on the sides, make sure you read through all of that material to glean as much information as possible for yourself. This is especially important if you haven’t had access to the full script.

Casting directors are auditioning you to see if you are right for the part, if you have an understanding of the material, and if you grasp the tone of the piece. They are not auditioning you to see if you know how to memorize lines. If you have trouble memorizing lines, you might think of finding another profession. I could always look at an actor and see in his eyes when he disconnected from what was going on in the scene. He would squint a little, trying to visualize the dialogue on that invisible page in his head, desperate to say the lines right. Then a downward spiral would ensue as the actor lost concentration, and the audition would become about the actor struggling for lines.

So ideally I would like actors to not use the word “memorize.” Memorizing always reminds me of learning a speech verbatim without actually understanding what it means. Instead, try to change the concept of memorization to *knowing the material.* Be as familiar as possible with it so you can make maximum eye contact with the casting director or reader. It’s fine to hold the script and glance down and grab a line if you need to, provided you never break character as you do so. Remember, at the end of the day the viewers would rather an actor glance down at the sides than disconnect from the scene to search their brain for the right line.

Many casting directors believe that odds are that the actor who never looks down at her sides during the audition will usually be the one who books the part. There’s no doubt she’ll get big points for being prepared. But that said, I would still strongly advise actors to adopt the term *know the material* rather than *memorize it.* Because if the actor thoroughly mines the sides to completely understand what is going on in the scene (i.e., specifically visualizing where it takes place, knowing what the relationships are, knowing what the character wants, and genuinely listening to what the other character is saying), the lines will come in a much more natural and organic way.

If you are going straight to producers for your audition or are in a callback or test situation, your goal must be to be off-book.

But it's best to still hold the sides during the audition just in case you have that blank moment. Again, the viewers would much rather you glance down at your sides and grab your line than watch you squirm and say, "Line," which distracts everyone from the moment. Also, walking into the audition room without your sides can send the message that you are at performance level, but you're not at performance level, because you haven't worked with a director yet. Holding the sides sends that subtle reminder to the viewers that this is still an audition. And if the actor never looks down at the sides, the viewers tend to forget that the actor is even holding them. In essence, the sides become an almost invisible extension of the actor's hand.

Of course, there will always be the audition for which the casting director asks for an actor to memorize the sides and be completely off-book. If this happens, by all means do it. There's generally a good reason. More and more, casting directors are recording all auditions for their producers/director, because productions are shooting outside of Los Angeles and New York. So casting directors have to send all the on-camera auditions to wherever the production is being shot and where casting decisions are made from those filmed auditions. In local markets as well, casting sessions are often recorded and choices determined from that one audition, with no callbacks. It's best in these situations to not be seen looking down at your sides, although holding them in your hand below the camera frame is acceptable, just in case. Actors must treat these "going on tape for producers" auditions as close to full performance as possible. (Ironically, "going on tape" is still the term used for this process, even though no one uses videotape anymore.)

1.3 What Should You Wear to the Audition?

After sitting through countless auditions and comparing stories with other casting directors, my best advice is that actors should always go into the audition room dressed with a suggestion of the character. First impressions are important, and from the moment you walk through the audition room door, viewers are deciding if you look right for the part. An actor needs to help the viewers visualize him in the role as much as possible, and dressing for the part is a key element of that.

When I advise an actor to go to the audition dressed with a suggestion of the character, I want to be clear that I don't mean go dressed in a costume. If you're auditioning for a policeman, please don't arrive in an authentic policeman's uniform with a badge. The better choice would be dark pants and maybe a work shirt. If the character is a doctor, don't come dressed in a white lab coat with a stethoscope around your neck; slacks and a collared shirt are all you need. Actors showing up dressed in full costume might be sending the casting director a message that they're too eager, too green, trying too hard, and/or are ready for only very small parts, overcompensating for being unable to handle a lot of dialogue.

When I mention this opinion in my audition workshops, I invariably hear the story about the actor who auditioned in a policeman's uniform and booked the part, and actually I have from time to time booked actors who were dressed in a full costume. But I can promise you that this generally happens only when casting small co-star parts. Once more, the safer choice is to steer clear of full-on costume choices and dress with only a suggestion of the character. The casting director will instinctively get that you understand who the character is and can now focus solely on your interpretation of the material, not your costume.

In **4.3 WALKING INTO THE ROOM IN CHARACTER?**, I discuss how I once held auditions for the part of a trust-fund bimbo junkie, a rich kid with tats and piercings, and how the lobby was filled with over-costumed leather creatures sporting tats on every limb and piercings in places you didn't want to know about. During those auditions I was relieved when an actress entered the room in torn jeans and a t-shirt, along with some small tattoos on each arm, a ring in her nose, and several earrings in her pierced ears. Her main focus was what the scene was about, not what she was wearing. She booked the part.

The flip side of wearing a costume to the audition is when an actor comes to the audition with no thought whatsoever about appropriate clothing or appearance. An actor who doesn't try at all to dress with a suggestion of character sends the message of being either unprepared or not caring about getting this part.

* * * * * * * * * * * * * * * *

While casting a pilot several years back, one of the series-regular roles I was looking for was the part of a male law assistant. As I watched hundreds of actors audition, I noted that most chose attire appropriate for a law office: dark dress pants and a collared shirt.

I called in for my producers an up-and-coming young actor who had been cast as the lead in about five previous pilots, none of which had been picked up to series. I knew his work and really felt he could be right for this part, so I had high hopes when his representation confirmed that he would be coming to the audition. When he walked into the audition room, my heart sank when I saw that he was wearing a white undershirt, torn jeans, and flip-flops. He said hi to everyone in a bit of an arrogant way and then shuffled into the room and plopped onto the chair. He proceeded to tell us he hadn't had time to look at the sides because he'd been too busy. Launching into a long and surreal tale (this story is detailed in ***9.6 No Excuses****), he finally began reading the scene mostly with his head buried in the script. The reading actually wasn't bad. In fact, it was pretty good.*

But when the actor left the room, the producers couldn't shake the feeling that this actor didn't care anything about their project. Even if he hadn't had time to prepare the sides, he at least hopefully had read the breakdown and knew the character worked in a law office. The fact that the actor looked like he had just gotten out of bed and couldn't be bothered to even dress with any semblance of character sent the message that either he was actually above fighting for this role and his talent should speak for itself, or else he had not prepared because this project didn't interest him very much.

So even as the search for this role became more and more intense, every time I asked my producers if we should bring this actor back in they said no. I had spoken to the actor's agent, who was pushing for his client to come back into the room prepared this time, but my producers were steadfast in their conviction; they just couldn't get past that first impression of the actor arrogantly entering their audition room in a t-shirt and torn jeans to read for the part of a law assistant. His antics and attitude had sent them the strong signal that he didn't really care about their project.

1.4 To Mime or Not to Mime: That Is the Question

One of the most frequently asked questions I get is what to do if there is a slap, punch, or kiss in the audition scene. Well, you definitely don't want to kiss thin air. Confusion reigns as to whether the actor should mime drinking a drink, eating, or picking up an imaginary object described in the stage directions.

The general rule is that **you don't need to mime unless the line doesn't make sense without the gesture**. For instance, if the stage directions describe that the character is sitting at a bar and drinking throughout the scene, but none of the dialogue in the scene refers to the character drinking, then there is no need to mime drinking. That would be extremely distracting for the viewers. However, if the stage directions say that your character throws a drink in someone's face and the other character's line is "Why did you do that?," then an action is necessary on your part so the line is motivated. It also shows the viewers that you understand what's going on in the scene.

If there is a lot of action in the scene, such as slapping or punching someone, it is necessary that your *intent* be to want to slap or punch someone. But punching thin air is usually too hard to make believable. I have seen actors in auditions make it work to punch or slap thin air, but they have to really commit to it; the tension in the actor's entire body has to reflect this deep desire to want to punch someone out. Moreover, because the actor is reading with the casting director or a reader and looking them in the eye, punching thin air while making that eye contact can make any suspension of disbelief difficult for the viewers.

When there's a kiss in the scene, it is indeed best not to mime kissing thin air with your arms wrapped around an imaginary person. I have seen that choice, and it is painful to watch. Your *intent* should be to want to be kissed, so no actual kiss is needed.

Let's say your character is driving a car in the scene. You don't need to mime steering the wheel; the scene is not about driving the car, and all that imaginary action will only divert the viewers' attention away from what you are saying. The scene is about what your character wants and how you're responding to what the other character is throwing your way. The dialogue is the most important thing in the scene, not the action of driving.

Stage directions might describe that your character is eating in the scene. The worst possible choice would be to mime eating your food with an imaginary fork throughout the dialogue. But if the line is "This is really delicious," maybe a taste off the finger or pointing to the delicious food in question could be all you need for the line to make sense.

And let's talk about when a gun is used in the scene. This is a hard one. The casting director has chosen this scene for you to read because she wants to determine if you can believably handle a gun. I have seen actors really make miming holding a gun work. It can be done, but it takes real visualization skills to pull it off. Sometimes the casting director will have a fake gun in the audition room to help you along (Note: Don't ever bring a fake gun into the audition room), but most of the time you're left to your own devices. If this is the case, then just remind yourself what it is you want. If you are completely focused on your intention (that you want to shoot this person), then you won't need to mime holding a gun to make your point.

The way you audition for a particular scene is not always going to be the way you will film it. The sides will often be full of stage directions and actions that are impossible to recreate in the audition. And if you try to mime all the stage directions, it will be distracting and look silly! Use your common sense to mime in the scene only if it is absolutely necessary to make the lines make sense. And if you do mime something, make sure you visualize it and commit to the action a hundred percent. A mime done lamely and halfway will only call attention to your lack of commitment.

1.5 Do You Ever Use Props in an Audition?

Over my twenty-three years as a casting director, I have watched many actors struggle when they choose to bring props into the audition room. They want to recreate the scene as if they are filming it, but they still have the pesky sides in their hand. How is it possible to handle the wine bottle, the glass, and the sides all at the same time? I have seen water bottles become a telephone, a pencil become a knife, and apples being munched. Purses have been brought in and used in the scene, as well as lipstick, towels, forks, knives, plates, coffee cups, bathrobes, tennis rackets, golf clubs, and lots more.

* * * * * * * * * * * * * * * * * * *

When I was Director of Casting for Movies and Miniseries at CBS, I watched a very famous older actress change clothes between each audition scene. This actress never should have had to come in to audition in the first place, but my bosses at CBS hadn't seen her act in a long time and were reluctant to just offer it to her. She really wanted the part and, champion that she was, swallowed her pride and strode through the doors of CBS with bag in hand. She set up all her different jackets, shoes, and hats off to the side, and between every scene rushed over to add to or change her outfit. All in full view of us, the CBS casting department. I was sweating by the end, but all her effort paid off. We gave Debbie Reynolds the part.

* * * * * * * * * * * * * * * * * * *

Most of the time, props are a major distraction from the dialogue and what is actually going on in the scene. We start focusing on your juggling of them and start to wonder how you're ever going to manage to turn the pages of your sides. An actor's goal should be to focus on the point of the scene and to ensure that the viewers are not distracted by too many antics.

In another example from the *Beck and Call* pilot, we were casting the role of Putsy, the head diva of a fashion magazine. Putsy fired assistants at whim, and the audition scene we used was chock-full of temptations to use props. I still love using this scene in my audition workshops to illustrate this prop trap and how an actor should handle it.

Take a look at the scene:

INT. CONFERENCE ROOM-CONTINUOUS

The 9:00 AM Senior Editors meeting is in progress. Cover layouts, cosmetic samples, and shoes are scattered on the table.

In contrast to Jemma's frantic subservience, her boss, Editor-in-Chief PATRICIA "PUTSY" MANNING, is at the head of the table—calmly helming her fashion publishing monocracy.

She's an attractive Asian-American woman in her mid-30s, the love-child of, say, Ralph Lauren and Vera Wang. Her work is her life and Lush Magazine, her child.

PUTSY

Okay, people. Two days and counting. Any updates on the benefit fashion show?

She looks to her executive assistant, CAROLINE LEEDS, 27 and just too skinny, too much makeup, and too eager.

CAROLINE

All three designers confirmed. Avi Maxwell called yesterday.

PUTSY

That's perfect. Nice job, Caroline.

Caroline smiles to herself, relieved. Putsy eyes a shoe she doesn't like. She sweeps her hand across the table, clearing it as though clearing her throat.

PUTSY

That pink shoe will never see the light of day. Can anyone tell me why?

Nobody dares say a word. She looks to Caroline.

CAROLINE

Lush announced beige is the new pink?

PUTSY

(cutting her off)

— which was the new white, which was the new gray, which was the new black, which is now O-U-T. So, make sure you show me beige, people. Not bone, not cashew, not wheat. BEIGE.

Jemma bursts in and sets the coffee by Putsy, who seems to ignore it. Jemma is painfully aware of the dropping temperature of the coffee. Putsy takes a bite of the omelet sitting before her.

PUTSY

Caroline, did you bring me this?

Caroline nods.

PUTSY (CONT'D)

How many people here knew I hated cilantro?

Everyone but Caroline raise their hands.

PUTSY (CONT'D)

Interesting. Caroline, would you mind picking up your things and excusing your-self from this room, this building, and this job? Human Resources is on two.

Near tears, Caroline picks up her things and leaves. Putsy goes to take a sip of her coffee. Jemma holds her breath.

PUTSY

It's good, Jemma...

Jemma breathes a sigh of relief. Too soon.

PUTSY (CONT'D)

But you know iced coffee hurts my teeth.

```
As Putsy pours the coffee into the trash ... Jemma
prepares to pick up her things and join Caroline in
Human Resources ...

                    PUTSY (CONT'D)
                     (discovering)
     Look! See my coffee people? THAT is beige.
     Thank you, Jemma. For pointing out the
     perfect color for Fall.

                      END SCENE
```

First of all, the role of Putsy had been written for Sandra Oh (before *Grey's Anatomy*), so I have left the original description of Putsy (Asian-American in her mid-thirties) in the sides. When Sandra could not do the pilot, my producers and the executives at Warner Bros. and CBS decided to open up the search for Putsy to any ethnicity and any age. (The relevance of this decision is discussed later in **6.2 You Are Not Wrong for the Part**.)

Second, this scene requires the actress auditioning for Putsy to do some miming and possibly use some small props to make the lines make sense. But trying to re-create all that descriptive action in the audition room by bringing in a ton of props would make for a distracting and unfocused audition.

* * * * * * * * * * * * * * * *

One actress ("she-who-shall-not-be-named") attempted to recreate all the stage directions during her audition for Putsy. This actress had recently finished a long run on stage in a high-profile musical. I was excited that she was coming in to audition and had high hopes that she could be "The One."

This "name" actress walked into the audition room with a large tote bag and, surveying the space, pulled over a folding table and trash can. She then removed from her bag a plate, a fork, a knife, a Starbucks coffee cup full of coffee ... and a pink shoe! My producers were so caught up in watching her send the pink shoe flying, use the fork to scoop up an imaginary bite of omelet, sip her coffee out of her coffee cup, and then pour the coffee into the trash can that they had no memory of how her actual audition was. No one could remember anything other than all her props and miming.

In trying to treat her audition as if she were filming it, the actress put too many distracting obstacles in the way of our actually being able to hear what the scene was about. We were so focused on the props, we began to worry that when she started pouring her coffee into the trash can she would miss and spill it all over the carpet.

* * * * * * * * * * * * * * * * * *

Several other actresses found the perfect balance when they auditioned for Putsy by using only a small prop to make certain lines make sense. For instance, a few came in with a Starbucks coffee cup (empty of coffee) and sipped the coffee during the line "It's good, Jemma ... but you know iced coffee hurts my teeth." They then tilted the empty coffee cup to pour the *imaginary coffee* out, saying, "Look! See my coffee, people? THAT is beige! Thank you, Jemma. For pointing out the perfect color for Fall."

Actresses who chose not to bring in any props at all were also successful in making those lines work by simply miming the action of sipping and then pouring out the coffee. Other actresses who chose to add no action at all during those lines, instead relying on their visualizations, were equally successful. But it was certainly not necessary (or a smart choice) to bring in a pink shoe to the audition; simply visualizing the offending footwear and pointing to it is all that was needed. And to also mime an imaginary fork going into the mouth and then chewing? Not a good idea. *Seeing* the omelet by smelling it or taking a taste off your finger will do the trick. Keep it simple. Remember, you can't audition a scene the way you are going to film it.

There is one prop that I do encourage bringing into the audition room: a cell phone. If you're on the telephone in the scene, a cell phone helps establish your place and relationship perfectly. It can also slip into a pocket easily after you finish with it. Other props that may or may not work, depending on how you've rehearsed using them, are purses, pens, and eyeglasses. Your script itself can become a lot of different things, and I love it when an actor's sides become a clipboard, a magazine, a map, or any number of objects. And if there's a lot of action in the scene, the sides can be used to make great sound effects if slapped on the leg or against a fist.

So when you are trying to decide if you should bring that prop into the audition room, remember that your audition is about what you are saying in the scene and what your character *wants*. The use of props runs the risk of distracting the viewers from your performance, and that's the last thing they or you want.

1.6 Preparation

Only once did I ever cast an entire miniseries by showing actor demo reels or recordings of their auditions. This was for the miniseries An Inconvenient Woman, *produced by Andy Adelson and directed by the Emmy Award–winning director Joe Sargent. Joe and I had worked together before on a movie-of-the-week called* The Incident, *starring Walter Matthau. My casting partner Randy Stone and I had won the Emmy that year for casting* The Incident, *so Joe really trusted me.*

With more than seventy roles, An Inconvenient Woman *was shaping up nicely with Jason Robards, Rebecca DeMornay, Elaine Stritch, Roddy McDowell, Jill Eikenberry, and Joe Bologna among the many fabulous actors. Joe Sargent, busy prepping for the movie, asked me to only show him videotape or demo reels for all the other sixty-plus smaller parts. Joe and I were so in sync that we quickly cast the whole miniseries that way and were ready to go.*

Just a few days before we were to start production, Joe had a heart attack and had to have emergency surgery. Fortunately he was fine, but he had to be replaced as the director. Larry Elikann, another award-winning director, stepped in and was shocked to hear that I had never brought one actor into the audition room for Joe! In an amazing display of leadership in a crisis, Larry had me recast only nine small parts. I held a casting session for him, and he was able to put his stamp of approval on the actors. Fortunately we got this done quickly and efficiently and did not get too horribly behind in our shooting schedule.

* * * * * * * * * * * * * * * *

I have heard that due to his special relationship with his longtime casting director Juliet Taylor, Woody Allen casts a good majority of his films the way we cast *An Inconvenient Woman*. But this scenario of casting every role of a project off recorded auditions is extremely rare and takes a very special relationship and trust between director, producers, and casting director.

That said, it is now commonplace to cast guest-star and co-star parts by viewing an actor's recorded audition. But for the most part, unless you are a star or are at the point in your career where you receive offers only, you're going to have to participate in that archaic audition process of actually appearing live in the room to get cast in a sizeable role.

Understand that you have chosen a career, and that career is *auditioner*. You will audition for more parts than you actually get cast in until you get to the level of being offered jobs. So unless you can figure out how to conquer the audition process, you will have a hard time accomplishing your goals.

Furthermore, auditions will often come through at the last minute, leaving you little time to prepare. Hopefully the sides will come at least the night before the audition.

When you first get your audition material, sit quietly and read it over silently to yourself. Make sure you read all the stage directions and figure out where the scene takes place, who you are talking to, what your character's intentions are, and what's happened right before the scene starts. Where the scene takes place can often determine whether you will stand or sit, or a combination of both.

Read the scene out loud, and if you aren't rehearsing with someone, read aloud all the other parts as well. Some actors have told me they like to record the other parts and play them back while rehearsing. It's important to place where all the other characters will be in the scene, including specific eyelines and choices about simple blocking.

If you decide that a mime and/or simple prop are necessary, make sure you rehearse this action so you'll be prepared in advance. Having just a vague idea about how you will do something in an audition (aka winging it) usually doesn't turn out so well.

You may think that getting the sides the night before does not leave enough time to prepare adequately, but with my simple set of auditioning tools you can be given the material even five minutes before and still be able to give a quality, informed audition.

In my audition workshops, I have developed **The 6 Audition Tools Method** to get the actor mentally focused and prepared for an audition. Perfecting the art of the audition process is mandatory for your acting career, and using the excuse that you're a terrible auditioner is simply not acceptable. The right tools will always help in preparing for the audition.

THE AUDITION BIBLE CHECKLIST

Before Your Audition

- ✔ Educate yourself as to who the casting director, producers, writer, studio, and network are.

- ✔ Read silently and slowly through the audition material for any and all clues from the writer.

- ✔ Figure out the tone of the show through common sense and research.

- ✔ Be familiar with the lines and material. Don't memorize; instead, know the material.

- ✔ Dress for the audition with a suggestion of the character.

- ✔ Make smart choices about miming and/or props.

- ✔ Get up on your feet and read aloud. Decide whether you are going to sit or stand in the audition (or a combination of both) and rehearse simple blocking.

The 6 Audition Tools Method

Tool #1: Sense of Place

Where are you in the scene?

Tool #2: Relationship

Who are you talking to or about?

Tool #3: Intention

What do you want?

Tool #4: Pre-Beat / The Moment Before

What happened just before the scene started?

Tool #5: Listen

What is the other character saying?

Tool #6: Respond in the Listening

Be present in the moment.

Chapter 2

The 6 Audition Tools Method

* * * * * * * * * * * * * * * * *

When the pitcher feels his foot on the rubber, his head should be cleared of all thoughts but three: pitch selection, pitch location and the catcher's glove, his target. Any intrusive thoughts should trigger the pitcher to back off the rubber and redirect his focus.

H. A. Dorfman
The Mental ABC's of Pitching

I always liken the actor to the athlete. The athlete must have mental discipline in order to accomplish the task at hand. "The tyranny of the scattered mind," writes sports psychologist H. A. Dorfman in *The Mental ABC's of Pitching*, can be the downfall of the pitcher. If the pitcher is thinking "a thousand and one things" other than his task, he needs to step off the rubber. The pitcher should only be thinking about three things: pitch selection, pitch location, and his target, the catcher's glove. If the pitcher focuses on these three simple tasks, he will be able to control his scattered thoughts and achieve mental discipline.

In my audition workshops at Holly Powell Studios, I teach **The 6 Audition Tools Method**. I ask the actor sitting in the lobby of the audition room to achieve the mental focus of an athlete by using the first **4 Audition Tools**, *sense of place, relationship, intention,* and *pre-beat / the moment before.* If the pitcher, as Dorfman advises, should only be thinking of three things to achieve focus before he steps on the mound, the actor should likewise be thinking of only four things to achieve focus before stepping into the audition room. The actor should consider himself the pitcher on the mound.

Once in the audition room and the scene begins, applying **TOOL #5: LISTEN** grounds the actor. Finally, utilizing **TOOL #6: RESPOND IN THE LISTENING** makes the actor present in the moment.

When these **6 AUDITION TOOLS** are used together, they produce real results in mastering the audition process.

2.1 TOOL #1: SENSE OF PLACE

Where are you in the scene? A prepared actor needs to convey a more compelling visual for the viewers than just *I'm in my office*, or *I'm in a grocery store*, or *I'm in my car*. You must get a specific visualization of the place the scene is set in. For instance, if it occurs in the character's office, you need a specific mental image of where the phone, desk, window, and door are.

The physical location of the scene will often determine whether the actor stands or sits in the audition. Is your character walking down the street or drinking at a bar? If the scene describes the character driving a car while talking with friends, the better choice would be to sit. Let the viewer know that you understand where the scene takes place, and visualize specifically what the car looks like.

One of the most confusing things an actor struggles with in preparing for an audition is how to deal with all those stage directions. Remember that you can't audition a scene the way it will be filmed, so be sensible about portraying a *sense of place*. For instance, if the stage directions state that the character is dying on the street, you wouldn't want to lie down on the ground during the audition, because that would be taking things too far. Simply slumping in a chair will give a suggestion of sense of place. The viewers can see your face and easily grasp what is happening in the scene and where it is occurring.

It's in the actor's best interest to stick as closely to the writer's intent as much as possible, but the stage directions do not necessarily need to be taken literally. If the stage directions state that the character is sitting on a couch but the dialogue has no reference to sitting on a couch, it's the actor's choice whether to stand or sit based on the character's *intention* in the scene.

In the five seconds before the audition starts, then, try to visualize specifically where you are in the scene as you survey the audition room. If you imagine the place through your mind's eye, then the viewers will see it too before you even speak your first line. If you're not specific as to place, the viewer may think you don't understand the scene, are not prepared, or worse yet, are not talented enough to create a compelling sense of place.

2.2 TOOL #2: RELATIONSHIP

Joy Sudduth was auditioning for the part of a lawyer on *Criminal Minds*. In her scene she was speaking to the judge, the jury, the witness, and the other lawyer, with the casting director reading all those parts. It was Joy's job to define the *relationship* of each character she was talking to in the scene and to get a specific visualization of each character. Not a generic "This is the judge," but how she actually felt about this particular judge. Did she like him? Resent him? Was she afraid of him? In clearly defining her relationship with the judge, she needed to find someone in her own life who brought up that same emotional response—an old college professor, a former boss, or even her father.

Let's say Joy's character resents this judge because he is condescending to her. As Joy thinks about that certain college professor who was always condescending to her, she visualizes him, and this image of her professor stimulates the specific emotional response of resentment. Now all Joy has to do is place this professor's face on the face of the reader to elicit the emotional truth required.

Using **TOOL #2: RELATIONSHIP**, Joy needed to repeat this process with the other characters in the scene, the witness, the other lawyer, and the jury. Let's say the other lawyer is someone she likes and respects, so when Joy tries to think of someone she feels that way about, her college roommate pops into her brain. Joy now uses those two different specific relationships during her audition: the condescending professor for the judge and the roommate she respects for the other lawyer. Even though the casting director is reading all the parts, Joy has distinctly different visualizations in her toolbox. It's a lot of fun when I see that an actor is visualizing a specific person to match the character being addressed. It makes the audition very personalized.

Susan Parks, a wonderful actress I worked with for a long time, came to coach with me for an audition. In the sides, her character was talking to her boyfriend and wanted him to do something for her. Susan had taken my audition workshop before and knew all about my **6 AUDITION TOOLS**. As we ran through the scene I couldn't quite put my finger on what was missing.

TOOL #1: SENSE OF PLACE was specifically visualized; it was also clear that the scene was between her and her boyfriend, so **TOOL #2: RELATIONSHIP**, was checked off; she definitely understood **TOOL #3: INTENTION**, what the character wanted from her boyfriend; and she began the scene in the middle of something, so her **PRE-BEAT**, **TOOL #4**, was working. After running the scene several times, I asked Susan if she had a boyfriend in real life. "Yeessss ...," she said, purring. I watched her body and face tilt slightly to the side in a coy, sexy way and could see her boyfriend's image in her mind's eye. "There he is!" I said. "Now do the scene again, and put your boyfriend's image on my face." Bingo.

Susan understood through doing her homework that the scene was with her boyfriend and intellectually understood how she felt about him. But when initially working on the scene, she hadn't been *specific* in visualizing someone in her personal life. When she thought of her current boyfriend, I could almost see his image in her mind's eye.

Relationship is not only who you're talking *to* in the scene, but who you are talking *about* in the scene. An entire scene can be about discussing someone who is never present. So if you don't have a clear understanding of what your relationship is with that person and a clear visual image, your audition will lack specifics. If I mention to you that my ninety-two-year-old mother called me from Dallas last night, I am visualizing my mother in my head as I'm telling you this story. And the tone in my voice when I mention my mother will speak volumes about how I feel about her. Your character need only mention another character's name once, and the viewers should be able to "see" that person and know just how you feel about that person. Let's say your character is hanging out in a bar with friends and your dad walks in the bar. Just by your character saying "Dad," the viewers should be able to visualize him and know how you feel about him.

Visualization and being specific are key. Even if you have the sides for only a short period of time, it is imperative to be specific about what your relationship is to the person or people you are talking to in the scene. This will save you when the casting director is reading multiple parts.

2.3 TOOL #3: INTENTION

Often an actor has not decided or hasn't gotten a clear handle on what the character's intention (what your character wants) is in the scene. When I ask actors in my audition workshops what the intention is, the answer sometimes might be "I don't know," or "I haven't decided," or "I'm confused by the intention," or it could be a long convoluted explanation. Keep the intention simple: *I want to change his mind,* or *I want to convince him I'm right,* or *I want her to like me.*

During one of my audition workshops, it seemed that **TOOL #3: INTENTION** was missing from many students' auditions. Or if not missing their choice was a bit off, or they were playing only one intention throughout the scene. **The thing to remember is that whatever the character's initial intention is at the top of the scene, it almost always changes during the scene**. That's what makes the scene interesting. It's also usually why the casting director has chosen this scene to read for the audition, because *something changes*. The casting director wants to see the actor change.

Maybe you've decided that your intention at the top of the scene is to punish your boyfriend for breaking up with you, and you've made the choice to be angry. It's possible the writer has even described the character as "yelling" or "angry." But if you play angry and yell throughout the whole scene it becomes tiring and uninteresting for the viewers; it devolves into a one-note experience, and you've missed the opportunity to explore a variety of emotions, nuanced manipulations, and different tactics. Your original intention to punish your boyfriend gets lost in a sea of yelling, and the discovery of a new intention in the scene is never realized. Always keep in mind that the character's intention changes in a scene based on circumstances or what another character says to you. And that's one of the essential goals of an audition: showing your range.

A writer has written these changes of intention into the dialogue to further the action of the story, and often the writer will use the stage directions to give an actor a roadmap. The stage directions may read "Joan is talking a mile a minute as she rushes to get ready for work." Use this description as a guideline for the tone the writer has envisioned, but don't take it to literally mean you should talk fast throughout the entire scene.

Let's say your character is going into a grocery store to grab some milk. **Tool #1: Sense of Place** is the grocery store. **Tool #3: Intention** is that your character wants to go to the store to get some milk. As your character is walking quickly down the aisle, she bumps into her ex-husband. **Tool #2: Relationship** comes into play. Now what is her new intention? It might be to get out of the store quickly and away from her ex-husband. The intention has changed in the scene.

In my audition workshops I discuss one of the 7 Universal Laws, the Principle of Polarity, which states that everything is dual, everything has its opposite, and opposites are identical in nature. Therefore emotions rise in dualities: happy/sad, love/hate, angry/calm—meaning we wouldn't be able to fully understand "anger" if we had never experienced "calm."

As an actor, it's your job to find the duality of emotion in the scene and make sure you not only understand that your character might be angry, but also recognize that calm is the flip side and needs to be explored. Once you hook onto your intention in the scene, exploring these dualities of emotion will not only infuse your audition with depth and range, but will help facilitate a smooth transition when the intention changes.

When working on an audition scene, it's your job to identify what the character's initial intention is at the top of the scene and just where the intention changes. The scene then has a beginning, middle, and end. Steer clear of making your audition a one-note scene.

2.4 TOOL #4: PRE-BEAT / THE MOMENT BEFORE

When an actor stands in front of the casting director right before the audition begins, this is the "make it or break it" point. If your thoughts are *I want to impress this casting director* or *I hope I do a great audition*, you aren't focused on the task at hand, and odds are your audition will get off to a rocky start. When asked, "Are you ready to start?," an actor's instinct is generally to please the casting director, and instead of taking a few seconds to get mentally focused, he'll dive right in and start the audition. *Don't want to keep the casting director waiting!*

The comment I remember most from producers and directors after an actor left the audition room was, "That actor was okay about halfway through the scene." That's because the actor did not focus on *the moment before* and jumped in quickly to start the scene. By not being in the middle of something before the first line, it took the actor a bit to warm up, by which time the viewers had likely lost interest.

One of the simple tools used to control mental focus in the audition room is **TOOL #4: PRE-BEAT / THE MOMENT BEFORE.** Be specific. If you can't figure out from the sides exactly what happened before the scene started, make something up. Mining the sides for as much information as you can get, as well as reading through any crossed-out sections of dialogue, can help you piece together the *pre-beat*. Take a look at the following description and the first line of the following scene:

```
INTERIOR BAR - CONTINUOUS

The friends hang out at their favorite bar, several
beer bottles scattered on the table. A game of pool
transpires in the background and the bar is lined
with the young, the well dressed, and the entitled.

                    JESSICA
     Donna, You can't be serious! Derek said
     that to you?! What a jerk!
```

The actress auditioning for Jessica may not know from the sides exactly what Derek said to Donna, but she will need to make up a scenario for herself. Possibly Derek said, "Donna, it looks like you've put on a few pounds." Or, "Donna, you're never getting my vote." Or, "Donna, I'm sick and tired of covering for you at work. I'm not doing it anymore." The viewers won't know exactly what was said before the line "Donna, you can't be serious!" but they'll recognize that the actor is in the middle of a conversation and having a specific thought.

* * * * * * * * * * * * * * * *

When I was working with Bob Greenblatt and David Janollari as their Senior Vice President of Casting, they had a deal with Alan Ball and were developing Six Feet Under *with him. Alan had recently finished shooting* American Beauty, *for which he won the Academy Award for Best Original Screenplay, and he told me a story about Annette Bening, one of the stars of that film. I don't remember what led Alan to tell me this story, but it has stuck with me.*

They were shooting a scene during American Beauty *in which Annette's character had to drive up in her car, get out, and then walk through the front door of her house, where she encountered some kind of situation.*

The director, Sam Mendes, turned to Annette and asked something like, "What was happening right before you opened the front door and entered the house?" Without missing a beat she answered, "I was looking at my blouse that I just got from the dry cleaners, and there is a spot on it!" If I am paraphrasing her exact words, you still get the picture. Annette's character had a very specific thought as she entered the house that was not spelled out in the script. There was no anticipation of what awaited her on the other side of her front door. She didn't just start the scene, she was in the middle of something.

* * * * * * * * * * * * * * * *

Before you say the first line of the audition scene, touch base with the first **4 TOOLS: SENSE OF PLACE, RELATIONSHIP, INTENTION,** and **PRE-BEAT**. And by taking five seconds to ask yourself, *Where am I? Who am I talking to? What do I want? What just happened?,* you'll begin the scene in the middle of something. Make eye contact with the reader … *and go.*

2.5 TOOL #5: LISTEN

Actors forget to *listen* when reading with a casting director or reader. Listening at an audition is sometimes challenging for actors, because they are used to working with other actors who give something back to them. But a casting director reading with an actor is usually just feeding the actor the lines, not trying to act, because that casting director is trying to watch you at the same time she's reading with you. Other times she might not be looking at you at all or, unfortunately, attempting to act, making things worse.

In response, actors tend to put up a wall between themselves and the casting director, expecting to get nothing back, so they end up acting by themselves. This leads to merely waiting for the casting director to finish speaking and thinking about how they're going to say their next line. The actor shifts into a technical performance instead of being in the moment and genuinely listening.

* * * * * * * * * * * * * * * *

My ex–mother-in-law, the wonderful Tony Award–winning actress Frances Sternhagen (The Closer, Sex and the City), *was doing a play in New York and was cast opposite a TV star to play her husband who had done very little theater. He barely looked at her onstage when they were performing each night, as he was so used to acting in front of a camera, more concerned about his best angle. It frustrated her greatly that she wasn't getting anything back from him.*

Frances had studied with Lee Strasberg, and to get through each performance she applied his "as if" concept: that an actor needs to find a specific visualization of someone in her own personal life to apply to her fellow actor. In this case, Frances visualized her co-star "as if" he were her current husband (who she loved) to bring up the correct emotions necessary for their onstage relationship.

Frances had also studied with Sanford Meisner and remembered his words: "When you aren't getting back from another actor what you need, you have to let the words be enough." So instead of listening to "how" her co-star was speaking every night, she listened only to the words he was speaking. The "what," not the "how." Using these two different teachers' techniques saved her every night onstage.

I was just starting to cast in the New York theater at the time Frances was doing this play, and I thought, "That's exactly what an audition is like! Actors never get back what they need when reading with a casting director or reader." They have to let the words be enough.

* *

The concept of "as if" had its roots in the Group Theatre in New York City in the 1930s and derived from Constantin Stanislavski's the System. Lee Strasberg advanced this technique in the 1940s and 1950s and named it the Method. Strasberg asked his actors to use *substitution* to recall emotions from their own personal lives and replace the circumstances in the script with their own.

Other members of the Group Theatre besides Lee Strasberg included Sanford Meisner and Stella Adler. Meisner broke from Strasberg to develop the Meisner Technique, best described as living truthfully under imaginary circumstances. Stella Adler also went her own way to create a technique that did not rely on the actor's own personal memories to create emotions but instead used the scene's given circumstances. She felt that drawing on personal experience was too limiting.

Sanford Meisner asked actors to be in the moment, concentrating on their partners. But when the partner was not "there" for you, he instructed actors to focus on the words themselves. That's what an actor has to focus on at an audition: to listen to the *words* the casting director is reading and be present in the moment. Don't listen to *how* the lines are read but rather *what* is being said.

The point to describing these different iconic acting teachers' techniques is that Frances Sternhagen had studied with both Strasberg and Meisner, and these amazing teachers had an obvious influence on her acting technique. When she found she had to save herself onstage every night, she called on both her mentors.

Listening to the casting director grounds the actor in the present moment. Comparing notes with several fellow casting directors over the years, we all agree the biggest compliment a casting director can relate about an actor is, "That actor was so present." The most interesting auditions are watching an actor listen, and believe me, it's easy to spot an actor who is listening, compared with an actor who is just waiting for the next line.

2.6 TOOL #6: RESPOND IN THE LISTENING

RESPOND IN THE LISTENING is my last tool in **THE 6 AUDITION TOOLS METHOD** I use in my audition workshops. Many TV and film auditions these days are recorded on-camera for the producers and director. It's important to remember that when your audition is on-camera, you are usually framed just below your shoulders. The reader is reading off-camera, and all that the viewers can see is you and your responses. **So fifty percent of a recorded audition is watching you *listen*.**

You must visualize the reader as the character you are talking to in the sides. This is where **TOOL #2: RELATIONSHIP** comes into play, and if it's used correctly the viewers watching the recorded audition will believe you are talking to the character in the script, not the reader. If you listen to the reader, responding to what is being said silently, the viewers will see a person who is present in the scene. The viewers should see the thoughts running through your mind as you listen to the other character(s) in the scene. *There is action in reaction.*

Trust me when I tell you that if the viewers of the recorded audition see a blank face as you wait for your cue, they'll skip right to the next actor. They can literally see when you're merely waiting for the next line and not actively listening, and after about fifteen seconds if they aren't grabbed by the audition, they'll lose interest. "Next!"

I love telling the story in my audition workshops about a one-line part I was casting in the pilot *Beck and Call*. The part was a coffee barista, and the line was in answer to another character's question, "Where's Oscar?" The barista's line was "He works at the 57th Street store now." That's it. One line. But what was unique about this barista role was that the actor had to use **TOOL #6: RESPOND IN THE LISTENING** for a full page of dialogue while miming making the coffee! I read the entire page of dialogue during the auditions for the baristas so my producers could watch the actors *respond in the listening.*

Remember that **TOOL #5: LISTEN** and **TOOL #6: RESPOND IN THE LISTENING** go hand in hand in making the audition successful. I read somewhere that during the taping of *Friends*, the producers always cut to Lisa Kudrow for reaction shots because she was so brilliant with **TOOL #6: RESPOND IN THE LISTENING**. All actors should go back and watch past episodes of *Friends* to see how Lisa uses this extremely vital tool to hilarious perfection. Consider it your homework.

THE AUDITION BIBLE CHECKLIST

The 6 Audition Tools Method

- ✔ **Tool #1: Sense of Place**: *Where are you?* Use visualization to imagine the physical location of the scene. Looking around the audition room, place exactly where objects are in this particular environment.

- ✔ **Tool #2: Relationship**: *Who are you talking to? Who are you talking about?* Decide how you emotionally feel about the other character(s) in the scene. Using a specific person from your life will bring up the appropriate emotions.

- ✔ **Tool #3: Intention**: *What do you want? What does your character want at the top of the scene?* The intention changes as the scene develops, based on circumstances or what another character says or does.

- ✔ **Tool #4: Pre-Beat / The Moment Before**: *What happened just before?* Make a decision about what happened or was just said prior to the actual first line of the scene. Remember, you are always in the middle of something.

- ✔ **Tool #5: Listen**: Listening grounds the actor in the present moment. Actively listen to the words being read by the reader; don't just wait for your cue.

- ✔ **Tool #6: Respond in the Listening**: Responding silently to what another character is saying is fifty percent of an actor's audition. Watching the thoughts go through an actor's head as he forms a response is often the most powerful part of the audition.

CHAPTER 3

THE LOBBY SABOTAGE

* * * * * * * * * * * * * * * * *

Your worst enemy cannot harm you as much as your own unguarded thoughts.

Buddha

3.1 SELF-SABOTAGE

I always say the audition begins in the lobby of the casting office—the same lobby filled with all those other actors bent on sabotaging you.

Truthfully, though, it's you who are sabotaging yourself.

You spy an actor across the lobby who you saw on television last night and who you assume has a lot more experience than you, and you tell yourself that you'll never get the part. Your inner casting director decides that the actor who just walked into the waiting area looks perfect for the part and will surely book it.

As you glance around, everyone reading for your part looks completely different from you. You start getting miffed that you were brought in for this role in the first place, since you are so totally wrong for it. The casting director comes out and hugs another actor and tells him how thrilled she is to see him and thanks him for coming in to read. On top of that, that actor is in the room for twenty minutes ... and you have to go in and audition directly after him. Furthering your anxiety, a group of actors are loudly bragging about having several more auditions later in the day ... and this is your first audition in six months.

Sound familiar? The voices in your head do a brilliant job of sabotaging your confidence, especially right before the casting director calls your name.

I have learned from every actor who's walked through that door—the good, the bad, the unprepared—and I've observed that the actors who were most successful in the art of auditioning were the ones who started getting mentally focused in the lobby, before they entered the audition room.

Earlier I mentioned that in *The Mental ABC's of Pitching*, sports psychologist H. A. Dorfman espouses that "the tyranny of the scattered mind" can be the downfall of the pitcher. Similarly, the voices in your head while you're sitting in the waiting area can sabotage your entire audition.

When you enter the lobby of the audition room, you're walking into a cacophony of sounds and distractions. You may run into someone you know, and your first impulse may be to chat and catch up. All too often you'll be laughing and exchanging stories when your name is called. As you enter the audition room you're unfocused, scrambling to get into the right "head space." Most of the time this scenario will result in a blown audition opportunity. As an actor you must adopt the mental focus of an athlete to combat distractions and sabotaging thoughts while sitting in that lobby, so when you enter the audition room you'll be focused and ready to go.

As you wait you need to get into your "bubble of focus," your "zone," or whatever else you want to call it, before walking through the audition room door. Not taking the time to get mentally focused, you run the risk of "the tyranny of the scattered mind" and tanking your audition.

3.2 The Bubble

Watch Michael Phelps in the moments before he dives into the pool. Observe the runner before the starting bell. Talk to the football player on the field, and he will tell you he doesn't even hear the fans screaming at him. Athletes understand that if they allow doubts and scattered thoughts to enter their heads that sabotage will overpower the task at hand and they will screw up. Wasn't it fascinating to observe Tiger Woods playing in a golf tournament post-scandal? The voices in his head certainly messed with his game!

The actor needs to view the audition lobby just as the gymnast would the gym floor the moment before hopping onto the balance beam or as the jockey would reining in his horse behind the starting gate. I suggest actors put themselves into a bubble of focus or zone to help achieve the mental focus of an athlete. I want the actor in the lobby to become the pitcher before he steps onto the mound, pushing away the thousands of inner voices.

Actors who have performed theater will understand this notion of the zone, which also applies when they are offstage waiting to make their entrance. They silently focus on where the play is taking place physically; what relationships their character is involved in; the situation their character is in and what they're going to do about it; and finally, the specific "moment before," so when walking onstage they are in the middle of something.

I read recently that Jerry Seinfeld uses the term "getting in the bubble" to describe the ritual he creates for himself while waiting offstage just before his stand-up performance. Jerry describes it as "a state of mind that a performer seeks before showtime, a few vital moments of calm before the tumult of an unpredictable live audience." This mental focus, the exact same discipline athletes employ, is what actors must master.

3.3 The Mental Focus of an Athlete

The mind thinks thoughts; that's the job of the mind. You will never be able to stop that process. But you can focus your thoughts by concentrating on specific tasks or tools, gently pushing random, extraneous, sabotaging thoughts into the background. While sitting in the lobby of the audition room, achieve the mental focus of an athlete by putting yourself into your bubble of focus and using the first four tools of **The 6 Audition Tools Method**:

Tool #1: Sense of Place

Tool #2: Relationship

Tool #3: Intention

Tool #4: Pre-Beat

Before your audition, it's imperative to have come up with specific visualizations that get triggered simply by touching base with each of these four tools. Just as H. A. Dorfman's pitcher thinks of only three things to help disburse random, extraneous thoughts (pitch selection, pitch location, the catcher's glove), the actor uses four tools to help tackle sabotaging voices: **SENSE OF PLACE, RELATIONSHIP, INTENTION, PRE-BEAT.**

While waiting in the lobby, if other actors try to chat with you or are talking loudly around you, just remove yourself to a corner. Remind yourself that you need the mental focus of an athlete; put yourself into a bubble of focus and concentrate on your four simple tasks.

3.4 THE LOBBY

Upon entering the audition lobby, you'll need to take care of a few things before you can retreat into your zone. The sign-in sheet is a necessary evil that (hopefully) keeps the audition running on time. If you're early for your appointment, take a breath and consider whether you're really ready to audition before you sign in, because if the casting session happens to be running ahead, you may get grabbed to come in before you've had a chance to focus. On the other hand, if the session is running behind, you might want to sign in quickly, since you'll have a wait.

Either way, the audition lobby can sometimes have an energy about it that is tense and can get your nerves pumping, especially if it is packed with other actors. By taking a quick glance around to feel the pulse of the room, you can gain control and begin the audition on your own terms.

Checking with the casting assistant to make sure you have the correct sides is always a great idea. Sides get rewritten all the time during the casting process, and nothing is worse than getting into the audition room with the wrong material. Some casting offices will put all the characters' sides on a table in the waiting area, so look around for that. I have known actors who will even read all the other characters' sides to glean as much information as possible about the script. (Note: That casting assistant is a future casting director himself, so make sure any questions or complaints are offered with respect. But that's something you'd do anyway, to anyone, right?)

If you run into actors you know, it's entirely acceptable to politely excuse yourself and ask if you can chitchat after the audition. They should thank you for that. Locate the best spot to wait where you can get into your bubble of focus. If a seat or corner is occupied, ask the assistant if it's okay to wait outside; that way the casting team will know where you are when your appointment time comes. Once you're settled in your spot, get into your bubble and focus on the first **4 TOOLS: SENSE OF PLACE, RELATIONSHIP, INTENTION, PRE-BEAT.**

When your name is called, you will move toward the audition door as a focused actor, ready to do your job.

THE AUDITION BIBLE CHECKLIST

The Lobby Sabotage

- ✔ Be aware of the self-sabotaging effects of the voices in your head while waiting in the lobby.
- ✔ Find the sign-in sheet and sign in.
- ✔ Check to make sure you have the most recent sides for the role you are reading for.
- ✔ Glance around the lobby and locate the best spot where you can wait.
- ✔ If you run into someone you know, politely excuse yourself and ask if you can chat after your auditions are over.
- ✔ Get into your bubble of focus and touch base with the first **4 Tools** of **The 6 Audition Tools Method.**
- ✔ Your name is called. As you move toward the audition room door, you're a focused actor, ready to do your job.

Chapter 4

Walking into the Audition Room

* * * * * * * * * * * * * * * * * *

I've missed more than 9,000 shots in my basketball career, I've lost almost 300 games, 26 times I've been trusted to take the game-winning shot and missed. I've failed over and over again in my life, but I still keep going out on the court. And that's why I succeed.

Michael Jordan

4.1 First Impressions

I'm sure you remember someone along the way telling you, "You don't get a second chance to make a first impression." When an actor steps through the audition room door, it is that first moment of visual contact that stirs visceral emotions in the auditors. It's that "thing," that indefinable something that's hard to put your finger on. When asked why I cast someone over someone else, my response is often, "I don't know; they just were it."

Actors must treat walking into the audition room as part of their audition. As discussed in **3.4 The Lobby**, your audition needs to start in the lobby, where you adopt the mental focus of an athlete, so that when you enter the audition room the people on the other side of the door witness a professional actor doing her job today. Putting the auditors at ease (or not) is accomplished within the first few moments of stepping through the door. Producers, casting directors, and directors all want to cast actors who are confident and comfortable in their own skin. They are searching for not only the best actor for the part but for a professional who is solid, present, and focused.

Example #1: Hilary Swank

Hilary Swank walked into the audition room and said, "Hi, Holly, nice to meet you." She looked directly into my eyes, and what I remember most was her complete presence in the moment. It seemed as if we had a job to do together, that we were a team and that I needed her as much as she needed me.

I first read Hilary for a few projects she didn't get. She became my new favorite actor, and I was so excited to be on the lookout for the perfect fit. Each time I brought her in she would ask for a little recap of her previous audition and why I thought she didn't get the part. She even started chatting with me about other auditions, prompting little strategy sessions about auditioning in general.

I called her in whenever a part was right for her, because I knew she would do a great audition, make me look good as a casting director, and possibly solve my problem by getting cast in the part. She knew she needed me to help her get past that "gate."

Hilary and I conspired about wardrobe, how much makeup to wear, and the personalities of the producers. She did end up booking a series-regular role in an ABC pilot I cast called Camp Wilder, *and I later also cast her in the lead of an NBC movie-of-the-week. We did have to troop Hilary up to NBC to read for the network executives, and I still credit Lori Openden, Head of Casting at NBC at the time, for approving an unknown actress to play the lead in one of their movies-of-the-week. But even then, everyone involved in the approval process knew Hilary wouldn't be doing television for long.*

Example #2: Sharon Stone

When my partner Randy Stone and I were casting My Two Dads, *we needed a love interest for Paul Reiser, the star of the series. We got a call from an agent about a wonderful new actress we didn't know, but the agent wouldn't let us pre-read her. We decided to trust the agent and let the actress come straight in to producers and read with Paul. Keep in mind that* My Two Dads *was a half-hour comedy.*

The first glimpse I remember is of a beautiful young blonde gliding into the audition room. She wore something white that billowed, and as the outside light framed her in the door, she was a vision. By the time she sat down in the audition chair, the room was hers; we were all mesmerized before she even opened her mouth. This was Sharon Stone. When she left the room, we were all a little speechless. We admitted she was not exactly a sitcom actress, but we all knew we had just seen someone very special. So a long discussion began about whether the writers could tailor the script to fit this actress and her brand of humor. Everyone agreed we should try.

Randy and I called the agent to let them know we wanted to hire Sharon for the part and that the writers were reworking the script. However, our excitement of "discovering a star" was short-lived when the agent called to say another project had surfaced that Sharon wanted to do more. I must say Randy and I enjoyed watching Sharon's career skyrocket and always credited our producers with giving it a shot.

Example #3: Leonardo DiCaprio

Another case of an actor walking into the audition room and making such an impression that the writers considered rewriting their script occurred when I cast a half-hour pilot called Quail Lake *that starred Bill Maher. I was looking for a seventeen-year-old boy who'd be the "older man" boyfriend to a fifteen-year-old girl. One of my favorite trusted agents, Darryl Marshak, pitched a young actor to me and qualified it by saying he was only fifteen but added, "He's so special you need to see him. Maybe you'll rewrite the script for him!" Darryl wouldn't let me pre-read the actor, but I again trusted this agent and knew he wouldn't send me anyone who would embarrass me in front of my producers.*

When the time came for this young man's appointment, I went out into the lobby to get him. He gave me a sideways grin, half adorable, half cocky, and I remember thinking he was way too young for the part. But as I brought him into the audition room and introduced him to the producers, his shy charm, self-confidence, and complete comfort with who he was won everyone over immediately. This was a young Leonardo DiCaprio.

I remember admiring how Leonardo brought his own personality to the part and didn't try to play "older." He was who he was, and his attitude was "Here I am, take it or leave it." When he left the room, my producers began an earnest debate about how they could rewrite the script so the boyfriend could be the same age as the girl. After much angst and knowing they were passing up an opportunity to be the ones who "discovered" this star, they reluctantly conceded that an entire plotline of the script could not be rewritten, even for this wonderful actor.

* * * * * * * * * * * * * * * *

As I observed how Hilary, Sharon, and Leonardo walked into the audition room, I couldn't help comparing this with the way other actors walked into the audition room. I'd watch an actor enter, looking down at the floor, not making eye contact with me, and I'd want to take his shoulders and shake them and say, "Don't you realize your audition is over before you even open your mouth?!"

The confidence an actor exudes when he steps through the audition room door is a necessary part of the audition process. The casting director senses immediately if the actor has that "certain something," that indefinable *presence*. This confidence, or lack thereof, determines whether the casting director wants to take the three minutes to read the actor ... or not.

Example #4: Naomi Watts

I was working on a movie-of-the-week called The Christmas Wish *and already had cast Neil Patrick Harris and Debbie Reynolds. I was looking for someone to play Neil's girlfriend and had already brought in several nice actresses but hadn't really hit on it yet. An agent called pitching me an actress who had recently moved from Australia to L.A. and said she was Nicole Kidman's best friend. I gave Naomi Watts an appointment for the next day but wasn't sure what to expect. Would this be just a straight-up favor or would this possibly be my answer to casting the part?*

My first impression of Naomi walking through the doorway was of a somewhat shy, humble, beautiful blond woman who seemed genuinely happy to be there. Her sly smile was endearing, and there was no trace of "diva" that I feared might come from the friend of a star. I read with her as she auditioned for my producer, Beth Polson, and I recall a very real, grounded, soft-spoken, confident, subtly sexy actress. We were drawn in and couldn't take our eyes off her.

I asked Naomi's agent to send over her demo reel so we could see how she looked on-camera and review some polished performances. I wish I could say that we all jumped to cast her right away, but the truth was that Naomi was an unknown for us. Her Australian accent was a bit in the way, although her American accent was very good. Somehow we managed to get clips of Naomi from Mulholland Drive, *a David Lynch film that had not been released yet. At the end of the day, Beth Polson, along with Lisa Freiberger, then V. P. of CBS Casting, decided to take a chance on this talented "unknown" and cast her. We were not disappointed. We all knew we were witnesses to a star in the making.*

Example #5: Demi Moore

It was 1985 and I was in New York City, and I had the luck to be the New York go-to casting person whenever an L.A. casting director came to town. This meant in a given week I could be working on a pilot, a feature film, and a movie-of-the-week all at once. I had already worked with Gail Eisenstadt, an amazing casting director who is not with us any longer, on the CBS miniseries Kane & Abel. *Gail had trained under the legendary Lynn Stalmaster, who almost single-handedly launched the new profession of "casting director."*

Gail called and said she was coming to New York to cast the feature About Last Night, *the film version of David Mamet's play* Sexual Perversity in Chicago. *Rob Lowe was already cast in the lead, and the director, Ed Zwick, wanted screen tests with Rob and the candidates for his leading lady. At the time, Rob was dating the actress Melissa Gilbert, better known for her television work on* Little House on the Prairie, *not film. Rob was happy when Ed decided to include Melissa in the screen tests, giving her a shot at the role.*

My excitement at being involved in such a high-profile project was quickly quashed when Gail revealed she had lung cancer. She swore me to secrecy and told me it was entirely possible that by the time we got to the screen tests with Ed she might be too sick to be involved. The plan was for me to be front and center from the beginning of the New York casting sessions, so if anything happened to Gail, Ed and the producers would be comfortable with me.

Demi Moore, one of the actresses we were interested in reading with Rob, had flown to New York for a screen test. We were holed up in a suite at the Le Parker Méridien hotel to conduct the auditions and screen tests. One of the scenes we were reading was a love scene between Rob's character and his girlfriend. Actress after actress sat on the couch kissing Rob and simulating what was going to be filmed as a nude scene in bed. I must say the scene with Melissa Gilbert got especially steamy!

When it came time for Demi Moore's appointment, I went to get her in her own room at the hotel, which happened to be right down the hall from our suite. I remember very clearly what she was wearing: a floor-length beige linen shift that hung down straight with no waistline, like overalls. She wore a white t-shirt underneath, and I immediately thought about all the other actresses that day who'd worn tight jeans and blouses to show off their figure. My first impression, and I couldn't shake this feeling, was that she was hiding something underneath her garment.

The chemistry between Rob and Demi was pretty fantastic during the audition; she was unique and fresh. Ed was filming the screen tests with his handheld camera and getting really close in for the love scene. It was hot! After Demi left and returned to her hotel room, Ed expressed concern that he didn't know what Demi's body was like under that sack dress. Because the actress cast would have a nude scene, he needed more information about what Demi's body really looked like. I was given the task of knocking on Demi's door and asking her to please put on jeans for Ed and come back to the audition room so he could...well... get a closer look. My nerves were spiking; I so didn't want to offend her with this news. "Shoot the messenger" was all I kept imagining.

As Demi stood at her hotel room door taking in my words, I could feel her obvious discomfort, but there was no anger there. She put her game face on and said she would be down shortly. I'll never forget how she strode into the Le Parker Méridien suite with a smile on her face, baggy jeans on her hips, and turned around for the backside view! It was then that she launched into a passionate plea and vowed she would lose twenty pounds if cast, promising she'd not let Ed down ... and talked herself right into winning the part.

As I observed over the years how Demi's body became her temple, admiring when she posed pregnant and nude for the cover of Vanity Fair, I knew that her having to put jeans on for Ed Zwick was a turning point for her and her career. And I was the one who had delivered the news.

4.2 Fake It Till You Make It

They call your name. The viewers are looking at you when you walk in to see if you are right for the part. First impressions are everything. If you walk in looking nervous or seem unprepared, they can spot it a mile away and don't want to take the three minutes to read you.

If you *do* feel nervous or unprepared out in the audition lobby, I want you to think of something you do in your own life that makes you feel confident. *Are you great at swimming, cooking, gardening, or playing tennis?* Watch how your body adjusts when thinking about this activity: Your shoulders go back, your chest moves from caved-in to centered. *Now* walk into the room. You see, behavior translates into thoughts. Your body language has sent the "confidence" signal to your brain so that you now actually start to feel confident. So as your body fakes confidence, your thoughts become confident. Fake it till you make it!

Treat walking into the audition room as part of your audition, part of the act. As you enter the room you need to be in a hybrid state, easily accessible to the viewers but also focused on your job. The good news is you're in the audition room for only three minutes ... *and you can do anything for three minutes.*

4.3 Walking into the Room in Character?

There are many theories and opinions out there about whether an actor should walk into the audition room in character. Some actors have told me that a coach had been adamant about entering in character, though another coach had advised them against that. Confusion about this seemed to dominate their whole audition process, and they were defeated about their reading before they could even make their way into the casting director's office.

What do I think? I can tell you without hesitation that you should not walk into the audition room in character. Walk in focused and ready to go, and say "Hello" or "Nice to see you," looking the casting director, director, or producers in the eyes. This could be the only moment during your audition where a little bit of your personality comes through. And just that "Hi, how are you?" can speak volumes about who you are as a person and convey whether you are arrogant, unprepared, nervous, or confident.

Once when I was being interviewed for a job to cast a pilot, the executive producer said to me, "Holly, if you cast this pilot, I want you to bring in only good citizens." I had never heard that from a producer before, but I knew what he meant. He didn't want me to bring in an actor who was on the "life is too short" list. He didn't want an actor on his set who would be disrespectful of fellow actors or who would gossip about the writing. He wanted to work with actors who would learn their lines, show up on time, and be team players.

So for this producer, the way an actor walked into the audition room and said hello was almost as important as the audition itself.

The Line Between Self And Character

When I started teaching my audition workshops and coaching actors, a manager I had worked with for many years called and said he was going to send me one of his clients for a private session. The manager was concerned because this actor had been working steadily for several years on great projects but for the last year had not booked anything. He wasn't even getting many callbacks. The manager asked me to work with him and see if he was doing something in the audition room that was causing this booking drought.

At the beginning of our session I chatted with the actor, asking him how he felt in the audition room and what parts he was mostly called in for. He told me he was usually called in to play assholes, terrorists, jerks, or the bad guy. I took a beat and said, "Do you walk into the room in character?" He answered, "Well, I never did until about a year ago when a coach told me I should." I then asked if when he chatted with the casting director and producers after the audition he did this in character as well. He paused. "Yes," he said. "Well," I told him, "that's why you haven't worked in a year. They think you're a jerk."

I explained that when the casting director, director, or producers chat with an actor after the audition is over, they're trying to get to know a little more about him and get a better feel for who he is. By his coming across as an arrogant jerk, these producers didn't want him anywhere near their set. The relief the actor felt when he heard he could be himself with the auditors was transformational. He was so excited. I watched his whole body relax as he realized he didn't have to carry on an act the whole time he was in the audition room. That same day the actor went to an audition and called me later to tell me he'd gotten an immediate callback. He was back to his old self: a working professional actor.

A Tale Of Woe

Here's an extreme example that should convince actors not to walk into the room in character: I was coaching an actress I knew well for an audition several years back, and the part she was auditioning for was a drug-addicted porn star. She was familiar with my tools of **SENSE OF PLACE, RELATIONSHIP, INTENTION** and **PRE-BEAT**. As I recall, the scene took place in a restaurant where the porn star was meeting with some producers about a film, and it included a confrontation about the porn star using drugs and the producers being reluctant to hire her because of that.

The actress created clear visualizations as to where she was in the scene, who she was talking to, and how she felt about each of these people (also having a specific visualization as to who she was talking about in the scene). Furthermore, she knew what her intention was at the top of the scene and understood that during the scene it would change.

We worked together for an hour for an audition later that afternoon. She left my studio feeling solid and with me convinced she was in control of her choices. About 6:00 p.m. that day the actress's manager called me to say that she'd just heard from the casting director of the project. I honestly thought the manager was going to tell me the actress had gotten the job. I was stunned when instead the manager related that the casting director was convinced this actress had actually been on drugs when she showed up to the audition. The manager wanted to know if I thought the actress had been high when she'd been coaching with me. I searched my memory of that morning to see if I had missed any clues that the actress might have been on drugs. I had worked with her for almost a year at that point, and I figured there was no way I wouldn't have picked up on something like that.

I called the actress, now in tears after being told of the horrible suspicion that she'd been high at the audition. I asked her if she had walked into the room in character. She said she almost never did but had decided to do it for this audition, because after coaching with me she felt it was best for her to just stay focused and in character.

The manager fired her. The agent fired her. The casting director never had her back into the office. They didn't believe her. She was a bit of a high-maintenance actress in any case, and I think this was the last straw; the manager figured that maintaining her own relationship with the casting director trumped her relationship with the actress. Of course, I can't be a hundred percent sure the actress didn't get high between our coaching session and the casting session. But my hunch has always been that she was actually just having a really great audition as she walked into that room.

Don't Scare The Casting Director

As I mentioned in **1.3 WHAT SHOULD YOU WEAR TO THE AUDITION?**, I once auditioned actors for the co-star part of a trust-fund bimbo junkie with tattoos and piercings. The scene started with the character entering a room and slamming the door.

About halfway through the day, as the lobby filled with overdressed leather vixens covered in tats and piercings, one actress decided she needed to stand out from the crowd. Instead of waiting for my casting assistant to bring her in, she flew though the doorway in a tight black leather Catwoman outfit, draped in chains, plus tattoos, piercings, Mohawk-spiked hair a foot high … and slammed the door. Hard. I jumped out of my seat, and when I realized after a beat that I wasn't being attacked by a crazy person, I got angry. I glared at the actress as we read the scene, and as she left my office I went out and announced to the other actresses waiting to please not follow that lead. The next actress who came into the room said all the others in the lobby had thought maybe they should all follow suit, that maybe that's what I wanted all the actresses to do.

Especially when auditioning for smaller co-star parts, an actor who walks into the room in full character sends a message to the casting director that she's green and inexperienced. The casting director wants to use professional actors in even the smallest parts. Being a professional actor means that you're able to transition in and out of character—during an audition, while rehearsing, or filming on the set. An actor who flies through the audition room "in character" is not only being way too theatrical for television or film but is telling the casting director loud and clear that he doesn't yet have the skills of a professional.

4.4 Don't Shake Hands

I know your mother taught you to shake hands when meeting someone, but in a casting session where many actors come and go, you can be sure some of them are showing up to the audition ill but don't want to miss this opportunity. Don't offer your hand for a shake unless the auditors do it first. Beyond that, if you go out of your way to shake every single person's hand in the room, it can come off as sucking up, and trust me when I tell you that disingenuously trying to score points is never lost on the auditors.

4.5 Taking Control of the Audition Space

I always say that part of the fear an actor experiences while waiting in the lobby of the audition room is fear of the unknown. You become anxious because you don't know what's waiting behind that audition room door: *What does the room look like? How many people are in the room? Is there a camera? Are the people behind that door in good or bad moods?*

A chair is the one familiar object that carries over from your living room (where you rehearsed the audition) to the actual audition room itself. While rehearsing the scene at home, decide whether you will be standing or sitting in the scene and if you will use a chair or not. The auditors usually have a chair in the audition space in case the actor wants to use it. So when you walk into the audition room, I want you to spy the chair. Touching base with the chair, whether you will be using it or not, helps to ground you making it "your space, not theirs."

Option #1: Giving Your Power Away

You walk tentatively through the audition room doorway, looking down and occasionally glancing up shyly at the people in the room, sorry to be invading their territory. "Would you like me to stand or sit?" you ask, avoiding a wrong choice or any risk of offending. The answer: "Ahhh ... just sit." This is an instant power giveaway. Because as you sit you're probably thinking, "Why did I ask that? I had rehearsed it standing when I was in my living room." Meanwhile, the auditors are concluding that you either have not prepared properly and need to be told what to do or that you're trying too hard to please. Even before the first line of your scene, you've made the viewers a bit anxious; they fear they'll be witnessing an actor winging an audition, rather than one who's prepared unique choices.

Option #2: Taking Your Power

You walk confidently through the audition door, saying hi to the people in the room, looking each of them directly in the eye, and then spy the chair. That's the grounding moment. Touching base physically or visually with the chair (the one familiar object from your living room) helps you claim your power and the audition space. It's now your room, not theirs. If chitchat happens and then it's time to start, turn to the chair and move it exactly where you want it. You can move it away, out of the audition area, or you can leave it just where it is. But it's your choice and decision. The auditors can see that you are prepared and have made a choice. They can relax a little and look forward to seeing what you prepared—and this is all before you speak your first line.

Of course there will be times when the actor's best-laid plans and preparation will not always go the anticipated way. You may have decided to sit in the scene, but when you walk into the audition room the casting director asks you to stand and not move much, because the audition is being recorded for producers.

Always try to find out ahead of time if your audition will be recorded, as this will often determine if you'll be standing or sitting and how much freedom of movement you might have. But usually if you are auditioning live for the casting director, director, or producers, you have a little more leeway as to how you present your material.

Chatting before the audition can also interfere with your momentum in taking control of the audition space. If you're focused and ready to go and the auditors chat with you first, just be sure to take a few moments to gather yourself before starting the actual audition, and touch base with **TOOLS #1-4**.

* * * * * * * * * * * * * * * *

Watching the way the wonderful actress Jessica Hecht (Breaking Bad, Sideways) *walks into and takes control of the audition space is like watching a ballet in progress. Often Jessica knows some of the people in the audition room, but is aware that chatting before an audition is not good for mental focus.*

On the other side of the audition table, producers and directors can get excited about an actor coming in and want to greet them warmly and chat, not realizing how it may interrupt the actor's process. I'm not sure whether Jessica is consciously aware of this or not, but she's perfected how to take control of the audition room without offending anyone.

As Jessica walks through the audition door, she smiles and says hi to everyone in the room, looking at each person individually. If she catches the eye of someone she knows well, she gives a special wave and in one seamless movement turns her focus to the chair, moving it to where she has planned for it to be. She then surveys the space to visualize where the scene takes place, taking a few moments to focus, and then turns to the reader and looks him in the eye when she is ready to start.

* * * * * * * * * * * * * * * *

Touching base with the chair in the audition room, whether visually or physically, is the building block that helps ground you in the audition room. Then by using **Tool #1: Sense of Place**, you will create specific visualizations. By taking control of where the chair is placed, you will have made it your space, not theirs. Remember, it's *your* three minutes.

4.6 Chatting with the Casting Director

You made it into the audition room successfully and are focused and ready to go with your choices. And then: (a) the casting director decides to chat a bit; (b) no one looks up at you; (c) they ask, "Do you have any questions?"

Many actors in my classes tell me how focused and sure of their choices they are when walking into the audition room, but then everything unravels because of something the casting director, director, or producer says or does. First, if the casting director, director, or producer starts to chat with you, this is a good thing. But many actors lose focus while the chatting goes on. So when the casting director decides chat time is over and looks at her watch and says, "Are you ready to start?," the actor feels the need to hurry up.

Don't let yourself feel rushed. When chat time is deemed over, make sure you take five seconds to gather your mental focus and remind yourself of your choices. Don't ask if you can have a moment to adjust (you might hear, "No, let's go; We're late"). Just take it. The asking gives your power away. Take control of the room yourself. It's *your* audition time.

If you walk into the audition room and no one makes eye contact with you, just make sure you're trying to make eye contact with them, so in that moment when they do finally glance up they see an actor who's focused and ready to go. Unfortunately, a habit of some casting directors is to then ask, "Do you have any questions?" This can throw off an actor's focus.

My best advice is to respond by politely, saying, "No, I'm good. Thanks." See, you've already made your choices, right? And besides, if you think you *should* ask a question and the answer you get back completely contradicts your choices, you'll more than likely spend the entire audition trying to make the adjustment on the spot. Honestly, casting directors would rather see what unique choices you have made and how prepared you are ... and then give you direction. They would rather see "wrong" choices than an actor struggling to adjust.

So skip asking questions unless you really have no idea what the relationship is in the scene or have no idea what is going on in the scene. Those are appropriate questions.

4.7 TAKE YOUR FIVE SECONDS

It's vitally important to begin the audition centered and focused. Chatting with the auditors, though helpful in creating a more relaxed audition room, can also distract from your concentration.

If chitchat happens (or not), when it's time to start the audition, get back into your bubble of focus. Take five seconds before you begin the scene to remind yourself of your **4 TOOLS**: **SENSE OF PLACE**, **RELATIONSHIP**, **INTENTION**, and **PRE-BEAT**. Look at the reader when you're ready to begin, especially if you don't have the first line. What the viewers want to see is an actor who takes control of the room and is mentally focused, prepared, and ready to go.

Sometimes actors can be their own worst enemies by overthinking things and letting those interior voices get the better of them. Here's an example of how an actor can let chitchat distract him, throw off his focus, and prod him to start the audition scene before he's ready:

CASTING DIRECTOR

I see you just worked with Jake Finbar. He's a great up-and-coming director.

ACTOR

Yes, he was fantastic to work with.

(VOICE IN ACTOR'S HEAD)

Things are going so well! The auditors are chatting with me like we're old friends! They recognized a name on my resume and are impressed that I've worked with this person! They like me!

CASTING DIRECTOR

(tapping her watch)

Are you ready to start?

ACTOR

Yes.

(VOICE IN ACTOR'S HEAD)

Oh no... I need to focus ... Crap, I was ready when I walked in the door then they started chatting with me ... I better start ASAP! Don't keep them waiting!

The actor's palms sweat slightly as he quickly fumbles to grab the chair, glances up to look at the casting director, looks back down at the sides to find his place, and blurts out the first line.

* * * * * * * * * * * * * * * * *

MORAL: The actor wasn't ready to start. He didn't take his five seconds to get back into the bubble and touch base with **TOOLS #1** through **#4**. There was no **PRE-BEAT** moment, so the scene just started and it took a page and a half of dialogue for the actor to get into the flow of the scene. By that time, the producers were looking at the picture and resume of the next actor on the list.

Here is an example of chitchat happening, but the actor remains mentally focused, not letting interior voices sabotage his task at hand:

CASTING DIRECTOR

I see you just worked with Jake Finbar.
He's a great up-and-coming director.

ACTOR

Yes, he was fantastic to work with.

(VOICE IN ACTOR'S HEAD)

It's nice they like the director I just worked with (smile and nod). OK, focus ... where is the chair? There it is.

CASTING DIRECTOR

(tapping her watch)

Are you ready to start?

ACTOR

Yes.

(VOICE IN ACTOR'S HEAD)

Where am I in the scene? Right ... my office. There is my desk and phone, the door is straight ahead, window to my left. Who am I talking to? ... my heartless boss. What do I want? ... a raise. What just happened ... I just hung up the phone from my wife who is pressuring me to buy a house.

As he turns to move the chair to where he wants it, the actor takes five seconds to touch base with **SENSE OF PLACE**, **RELATIONSHIP**, **INTENTION**, and **PRE-BEAT**. Using specific visualizations, he makes eye contact with the reader and says the first line.

* * * * * * * * * * * * * * * * * * * *

MORAL: The actor was pleasant but focused while relating to the viewers. He took control of the audition room, knowing it was his three minutes. Using **TOOLS #1** through **#4** to help visualize his office, the actor conjured a specific mental image of his boss, focused on wanting a raise, and had his wife's voice ringing in his ears. So as he looked up at the reader and began the scene, the actor was in the middle of a thought.

4.8 Leaving the Audition Room

After your reading is over, leave with as much confidence as you had when you came into the room even if you felt your audition was less than stellar. If you dash out, looking down, mumbling good-bye, they might believe you thought you didn't do a good job and may dismiss you. But if you walk out slowly with confidence, they may think that you're a solid actor who may have had a bad moment in your audition. With this, the likelihood increases of them asking you to do it again before you get all the way out the door.

When you finish the audition, take a few beats to come out of the scene, just as you took a few beats to start the scene. This is often one of the most awkward moments in the audition. You've made your choice, and the viewers are assessing what they saw.

A good option before leaving the room is to look each person in the eye and ask, "Anything else?" This gives everyone a beat to decide, and if they say, "No, that's good, thanks," or don't say anything, then take control and exit the room saying, "Okay, thanks," or "Nice to see you," or something brief. Never say, "Thanks for the opportunity," or anything that implies you're someone who doesn't belong there.

I'm not suggesting you be jubilant if you didn't think your audition was very good, but do put an upbeat twist on your exit, even if you thought you sucked. The exit is part of your entire audition and an important skill to master.

It might be hard for you to, say, stick to a diet for a month, or after a tortuous twenty-four hours not call that boyfriend who broke up with you, or keep your New Year's resolution to go to the gym every morning for six months, but for three minutes you can summon the mental focus to do just about anything.

From the time you walk into the audition room until you walk out of that room, maintain the mental mindset of the athlete.

It's only for three minutes. And remember...*you can do anything for three minutes.*

THE AUDITION BIBLE CHECKLIST

Walking into the Audition Room

- ✔ Walk into the audition room with confidence.
- ✔ Fake it till you make it.
- ✔ If chitchat happens, stay focused.
- ✔ Spy the chair. It's your room, not theirs.
- ✔ Glance around the room to visualize where you are in the scene, establishing your sense of place
- ✔ Are you ready to start? Take your five seconds.
- ✔ Look at the reader when you're ready to start.
- ✔ Leave the room with as much confidence as when you entered.

CHAPTER 5

THE READER

* * * * * * * * * * * * * * * * *

Listening never happens in the past or the future.

Gregory Kramer

5.1 VISUALIZATION

The biggest difference between doing an audition and doing a scene in acting class is that in acting class you are working with another actor, and in an audition you are reading with the casting director or a reader whose job is to feed you the lines, not act the part (well, hopefully they won't try to act).

In the throes of an audition, if you only "see" the casting director reading opposite you instead of *visualizing* the character who's in the scene, more than likely your audition will become technical and nonspecific. Or worse, your audition will be thrown completely if your thoughts turn to impressing the casting director instead of what is going on in the scene.

If the audition sides depict a scene about two people who are attracted to each other, you're going to have a hard time diving into the scene in a truthful way if you use only the casting director or reader as the object of your affection.

This makes **TOOL #2: RELATIONSHIP** especially important to get a clear grasp on. It's imperative to have a strong visualization of the person in the sides you're supposed to be attracted to—and not just what that character might look like, but who specifically in your own life you're attracted to, so it brings up the proper emotion in the scene.

* * * * * * * * * * * * * * * *

I cast a series for five years called One on One *that was on the UPN Network, now folded into the CW Network. Our stars were Flex Alexander and Kyla Pratt, and the show was about a single dad raising a teenage daughter. I had to cast a lot of boyfriends as guest stars to play opposite Kyla. The difference I found between auditioning adults and teens is that teens can still embrace the sense of play and unleash their imaginations more easily than adults. The blocks haven't piled up yet in their young lives.*

As I auditioned these teenage boys, I often found myself blushing while reading with them. This happened so often that my producers, Bob Greenblatt and David Janollari, once said, "Holly, your husband better watch out! You're going to run off with a fifteen-year-old boy!" You see, these kids had visualized the young and adorable Kyla Pratt so clearly and put that visualization on my older-woman face that when they looked at me it felt like the real thing!

* * * * * * * * * * * * * * * *

When using visualization in the audition room, your goal is to choose a specific person in your own life who brings up the correct relationship in the scene. If you don't have anyone in your own life for a particular circumstance, then look to friends, a film, a book, or whatever substitution works. By placing a specific visualization on the casting director or reader's face, your audition is sure to be more grounded and truthful.

5.2 Two or More Characters in Your Sides

One of the biggest challenges in the audition room is having to read with a casting director or a reader who is sometimes covering two or more different parts. When you're working on a scene in acting class, other actors are playing the various parts, and when you're actually cast in a project you can rely on fellow professional actors to help create the reality of the scene.

It is common for audition material to include two or more characters that your own character is speaking to, especially in episodic casting; guest star and co-star parts in an episode of television are usually written to interact with multiple characters.

First you must determine what the different relationships are in the scene and summon specific visualizations for each of the different characters. Using **Tool #2: Relationship** will not only make the audition specific but will prevent confusion on the viewers' part as to who you're talking to, moment to moment. Planning ahead where to place the various characters is imperative, and this is especially important when your audition is on-camera. When done correctly and specifically, the people viewing the recorded audition will be able to visualize all the various characters you're speaking to. **5.4 Cross Camera** delves into more detail on this subject.

5.3 EYE CONTACT / EYELINE

Use the casting director or reader as the main person you're speaking to in the scene. If another character enters the scene, it's fine to look off and "see" that person entering, making sure your eyeline is always in a certain spot. Let's say in the scene that you are on a date, and you are using the reader as your date. A waiter enters and asks, "Are you ready to order?" If you have only one or two lines with that waiter, directing your lines into thin air is fine. Then you look back to the reader as your date and resume your conversation. Remember, you have a different relationship with the waiter than you have with your date, so this gives you the opportunity to establish two different relationships. And if you've done your visualization homework, it will be clear to the viewers that you're talking to two different people.

But don't get caught doing an entire scene into thin air. If there is a long conversation with the waiter, at some point you are going to want to bring your focus back to the reader. Establish the eyeline where the waiter is standing and then with your eyes follow that waiter to where the reader is, as if the waiter is walking across the room. Remember, if the audition is on-camera only the actor auditioning will be seen, not the reader. If you are consistent and specific with different eyelines, it will look very believable to the auditors watching the audition that you are engaged with different characters.

Make sure you choose the same spot consistently when placing a character's eyeline. Nothing throws an audition quicker than when an actor establishes an eyeline in a certain spot and delivers the next line to a spot five inches downward.

Always make as much eye contact with the reader as possible. But as discussed in **1.2 Memorization**, the viewers would rather see an actor hold the sides during the audition than watch a struggle for lines. While holding the sides you can still glance down and grab a line if needed and come right back and make eye contact with the reader. The ultimate goal is to be so connected to the reader that the sides become an extension of your hand, and for the viewers, the sides disappear.

If you are doing a monologue, you will not be reading with a reader, and in this situation the viewers don't like to be used as the character you are speaking to. In this case, pick a particular spot on the wall or in thin air and place your visualization of the character you're addressing in that same spot throughout the monologue. Being consistent with your eyeline is crucial to believability.

Just a reminder, in case you are reading this book out of sequence: I usually refer to the norm for theatrical auditions, which means auditions for television and film, not commercials. Commercials often have their own rules about eyelines and where an actor should look if there are multiple characters in the commercial copy. However, my **6 Audition Tools Method** can be applied to most auditions anywhere—TV, film, theater, webisodes, and so on.

5.4 CROSS CAMERA

When you are going on-camera for an audition, the reader will be sitting close to the camera so that the viewers of the recorded audition can see as much of the actor's face as possible. The actor will be framed fairly closely, usually at shoulder level. As stated earlier, always use the reader as the main character in the scene, making direct eye contact with that person.

When a second character enters the scene (let's say the waiter asking, "Are you ready to order?"), the perfect actor choice would be to place the waiter *on the other side of the camera* from where the reader is sitting. If the reader is sitting just to the right of the camera and reading the part of the date, the waiter should be placed just to the left side of the camera: *cross camera*. Then when the waiter says his line, "Are you ready to order?," the actor can look up to the left, establishing the eyeline of the waiter standing to the left side of the table. As the recorded audition is watched, it will look very believable that the actor is talking to two different people in two different places.

To wrap up: It's not unusual to have two or more characters in audition sides. It is your job to plan ahead of the audition just where you'll place each of these characters. Again, the main character in the scene should be the reader. When a second character comes in, try to place the new character cross camera, on the opposite side of the camera from where the reader is sitting. If a third character comes in, make sure you establish a new eyeline for that person, again using the cross camera technique. Creating a consistent eyeline and a specific location is imperative for each new character.

5.5 GOOD READER, BAD READER

Bored reader. Slow reader. Speedy reader. Never-looks-at-you reader. Aspiring-actor reader. New York–accent reader. Nasal reader. No, this isn't a passage from a new Dr. Seuss book. This is just a small list of the types of reader personalities you may encounter on your auditions.

How many times over the years have I heard actors say, "That casting director reading with me completely threw my audition!" You will *never* get back from a reader what you get when working with another actor, so don't expect to. Once you start the scene, your mental focus should only be to *listen* (**2.5 TOOL #5: LISTEN**). Like the pitcher who steps on the mound and focuses on the catcher's glove, the actor's focus should be on listening to the reader.

It's entirely possible that the reader is a bad reader, not looking at the actor, or worse, trying to act. If you allow yourself to fall into hearing *how* the reader sounds, you will destroy your mental focus.

I've heard so many actors complain that the casting director never even looked up during the entire audition. It is true that casting directors read with actors all day long, and they get tired. They are human too, believe it or not. But what they are longing for is the actor who will walk into the audition room, grab their attention, and force them to look up from the script. They want to find that actor who will save their day.

* * * * * * * * * * * * * * * * * * *

I was at one of the networks testing actors for a series-regular role on a pilot. We were reading a love scene between the actors we were auditioning and their character's female lover. The reader happened to have a very nasally voice and pronounced New York accent. I remember being concerned that the reader's voice would throw the actors testing. But all three actors we were testing were pros, and I learned something that day about a professional actor's mental focus in the audition room. Not one of them was thrown by the reader's voice, because they so clearly not only had a specific visualization for their lover, using **TOOL #2: RELATIONSHIP,** *but their visualization of their specific lover included the sound of her voice.*

* * * * * * * * * * * * * * * *

Do you remember the story in **2.5 TOOL #5: LISTEN**, about my ex–mother-in-law, Frances Sternhagen? She was doing a Broadway play in New York with a television actor playing her husband who never looked at her onstage during the entire performance. She said in order to save herself she had to use "as if" every night. That included using visualizations for not only the mental image of a husband she loved but for the sound of his voice as well.

All three actors at that network audition used "as if" to save themselves. As Sanford Meisner said, *When you aren't getting back what you need from another actor you have to let the words be enough.* Not *how* the words sound, but what the words are. Listen to the words. This mental focus on listening grounds you into the present moment. And the biggest compliment a casting director can give is to say, "That actor was so present in their audition." It's because the actor was mentally focused on the simple task at hand and truly *listening*.

The professional actor will never let a bad, bored, or speedy reader throw an audition.

THE AUDITION BIBLE CHECKLIST

The Reader

- ✔ You are usually reading with the casting director or a reader who is feeding you the lines. Not a fellow actor.
- ✔ Use **Tool #2: Relationship** to get a specific visualization of someone in your own life who brings up the correct emotion called for in the scene.
- ✔ Place that specific visualization on the reader's face.
- ✔ Make as much eye contact with the reader as possible.
- ✔ If the reader is reading multiple parts, create specific visualizations for each of the different characters in the scene, again using **Tool #2: Relationship**.
- ✔ Establish the correct eyeline for each of the different characters you're speaking to in the scene.
- ✔ Don't get caught doing an entire scene into thin air.
- ✔ Use cross camera to help establish where different characters are in the scene.
- ✔ Don't listen to how the reader sounds, listen to the *words being said.*

Chapter 6

Demystifying the Audition Process

* * * * * * * * * * * * * * * * * *

Acting is not about being someone different. It's finding the similarity in what is apparently different, then finding myself in there.

Meryl Streep

6.1 Don't Try to Figure Out What "They" Want

As soon as you get your sides for an audition, we have discussed how you should first mine them: *Where are you? Who you are talking to? What do you want?* The second thing you need to determine is the *tone* of the script. The third thing actors often do (and shouldn't) is try to figure out what the auditors are looking for. This trap of trying to sneak inside the head of the casting director, producer, or director for the magic bullet of what "they" want is a slippery slope and can lead to a boring, one-note audition.

You see, the truth is, "they" don't always know what they want. "They" are waiting for an actor to come in who will show them what they want. How often when discussing with producers what it is they're looking for have I heard, "I'll know it when I see it."

I have lost count over the years when casting TV pilots or episodes how many times the original description of a character changed drastically after a certain actor came into the audition room. The writers with their big black pens changed the description to match the actor.

One of the big differences between casting television and theater is that in television the writers are alive and well and in those rooms with their big black pens. In theater, frequently the writers are, for lack of a better word, dead or not invited to the casting. Also in theater, characters are typically set in stone so that actors must fit themselves into the part and search for similarities. But the beauty of television casting is that it is a *personality-driven business*. While not compromising the script, actors have the freedom to bring their own personality to the part and make it work for them.

Let's say I read fifty actors in a day for the same part. Very often forty-nine of them will read the sides in a strikingly similar way. The tragedy is that these actors have squashed their own original instincts about the part by trying to second-guess what they think the auditors are looking for. Fearing being wrong with their unique takes, they end up making safe, middle-of-the-road choices. And a middle-of-the-road audition is bland and boring and certainly not memorable. As I always say, "Nice and fine does not get the part."

It's that fiftieth actor who walks into the room, bringing a unique interpretation to the part, who will likely book the part. That uniqueness is his or her own personality.

I always prefer an actor to show me what she prepared first, even if the choice is "wrong." I can see her unique take on the material and can then direct her if I need to. In a best-case scenario, the actor shows me something about this character that no other actor has thought of ... and just maybe the writers will use their big black pens to rewrite the part to fit her.

6.2 YOU ARE NOT WRONG FOR THE PART

All too often actors will get an audition and immediately sabotage themselves by telling themselves they are not right for this role. They spend precious time getting upset with their agents for sending them in on something that is so obviously wrong for them. Please know that casting directors are not going to waste time bringing you in to read if you don't have the potential to book the part. They have seen your picture or know you already and have called you in for a reason.

* * * * * * * * * * * * * * * *

I'll never forget when a fairly well known actress came in to read for a pilot I was casting right after we had adjusted the character's age range up by ten years. To my surprise (I'd had this actress in to read for producers many times before), she walked into the audition room and angrily said, "Holly, why did you call me in on this? Every other actress in the lobby is ten years younger than I am. I'm not right for this!"

After my shock that she had pretty much revealed her age to a roomful of producers, I calmly stated that we had adjusted the possible age range of the character. The character was originally written to be just a year or two out of college. When the producers couldn't find anyone they liked in the younger age range, they said it would be easy to rewrite the character to be out of college a little longer, since that point had nothing to do with the storyline. With the stroke of a pen, the character could now be late twenties, not early twenties. But this actress obviously didn't even consider this possibility and thought I was making her look bad. My main point is that the actress should have trusted me, the casting director, to not bring her in if I didn't think she could be right for the part. She decided she knew better, and instead of making herself right for the part, the result was a missed opportunity for everyone.

6.3 Bringing Your Own Personality to the Part

One night an actress in class pulled me aside to tell me how upset she was because she had been given a callback for what was described as "an overweight secretary." She was really stressing that she was being viewed as fat and asked me if I thought that as well. As I looked over her lovely slim body, I knew immediately what that casting director was doing. This actress was attractive, but in television-land, she was considered a character actress. Keep in mind that this was a co-star part of about five lines whose purpose in the script was to further the plot in some way.

I explained to the actress that this part was probably added to the script at about 3:00 a.m. The writer was trying to send the message that they wanted a character actress for this secretary (not a beautiful-model type) by using the shorthand description "overweight." The actress later told me that when she went to the callback, she was the only actress in the lobby who was not overweight. She booked the part. By not having every actress who read for this secretary be overweight, the casting director had thought outside the box and saved the writers from themselves by not casting "on the nose."

Here's a great example of the original description of a character changing drastically. I was casting the pilot *Beck and Call*, written by Dan Bucatinsky. As I mentioned in **1.5 Do You Ever Use Props In An Audition?**, the role of Putsy, the head of a fashion magazine, was originally written for Sandra Oh. The description in the script read as follows:

```
PATRICIA "PUTSY" MANNING is at the head of the
table calmly helming her fashion publishing
monocracy. She's an attractive Asian-American woman
in her mid-30s, the love child of, say, Ralph
Lauren and Vera Wang. Her work is her life, and
Lush Magazine her child.
```

Early on in the casting process I was told that Sandra Oh was unable to do the pilot. I remember when Lisa Kudrow and Dan, my producers, called me in to tell me the news. After a brief discussion about other Asian actresses, they said, "Okay, now we can open up Putsy to be any age or any ethnicity!" After all the color drained from my already pale face, I swallowed and said, "No problem!" That meant I needed to bring in every actress in Hollywood.

You see, Putsy was the head of a fashion magazine and her age or ethnicity didn't have anything to do with the storyline. It was the quality of a diva we were looking for, and that could come in all shapes, sizes, ages, and skin colors. So off I went and re-released the breakdown of the character of Putsy to all the agents and managers in town—"Any age, any ethnicity"—leaving out the original description of Putsy being Asian and in her mid-thirties.

After reading tons of actresses from Sandra Bernhard to Jamie Lee Curtis to China Chow, we ended up casting Vanessa Williams. But that original description of Putsy remained in the script (Asian, mid-30s). I love giving this scene out in my audition class to a fiftyish Caucasian woman to see how she handles it.

As an actor, it's important to treat every audition as an opportunity to show what you can bring to the table. By bringing your own personality to the part, you can ultimately make it work for you, and who knows, those writers in the room just may have to use their big black pens to adapt what they wrote to suit you.

6.4 Don't Go to the Audition to Get the Part

I want to turn the conversation back to the mental focus of the athlete for a moment. If the pitcher stepped onto the mound with his only thought that he wanted to win the game, I would lay bets he would probably throw a ball as opposed to a strike. Likewise, an actor who walks into the audition room thinking only of booking the job will likely turn in a technical performance, anticipating every thought, and will not be present in the moment.

"I hope I book this part" is a sabotaging thought that interferes with the actor's mental focus and stands in the way of a job properly done. Many times after I've coached an actor for an audition with reminders of the **4 TOOLS**: **SENSE OF PLACE, RELATIONSHIP, INTENTION,** and **PRE-BEAT**, the actor walks out the door and says, "I hope I get it." That's when I pull that actor back into the room and say, "Hold on. You're not ready yet."

Again, an audition is your chance to act today and show your best work to a casting director, director, or producer. And if you're doing your job properly the people on the other side of the table, who might not think you're quite right for *this* part, will think of you for other parts or other projects in the future. If you deliver a present and alive and unique audition, the casting director will be thrilled and excited to have discovered their "new favorite actor." Trust me, we can't wait to have another project to bring a terrific actor in on. Every casting director will tell you that this act of discovery is the most exciting thing about being in casting.

I remember the goosebumps I'd get when I discovered a special actor during an audition. Sure, probably the agent sent him to me, maybe an acting teacher told me about her, or I pulled the picture myself for a pre-read, so I didn't truly "discover" them, but those particular actors were new to me and starting out, and I was there to witness the magic. This happened with Hilary Swank, Reese Witherspoon, Naomi Watts, Ryan Reynolds, Stephen Dorff, Mercedes Ruehl, Alicia Silverstone, Kyle Chandler, Tina Majorino, Charles "Chip" Esten, and George Eads, to name a few of the wonderful actors I had the privilege to cast early in their careers.

After Hilary Swank auditioned for me the first time, I couldn't wait to find the next project I could bring her in on. She became my "new favorite actor," and I booked her quickly in her first series-regular role in a television show called *Camp Wilder* and shortly after that in an NBC movie-of-the-week. Seven years later Hilary was cast in *Boys Don't Cry* and, well, you know the rest. Hilary showed up at each audition with the attitude that it was yet another aspect of building her career ... not necessarily to book the part she was reading for.

There are so many things out of your control that determine why you might not book a part – your height, your skin color, your age. You have absolutely no control over those three things. The leading man already cast could be 5'7" but you're 5'11" and not going to be a good fit for him. If a family is being matched up, you may be hands down the better actor, but your skin color is too light or too dark to match the parents already cast. I'm sure you have gotten the feedback many times: "Good actor, but too young," or "Good actor, but too old," or "Good actor, but not right."

Don't spend hours or days after the audition trying to second-guess why you didn't get the part. That will only drive you crazy.

Remember that the casting director has pressures that may be as mundane as making sure there are not two blond actresses in the show or that the supporting actor looks nothing like the lead actor. Or pressures more complicated, like trying to please the producers, the studio, and the network who can't agree on choices for the cast. The next time you walk into an audition room and get that dirty look from the casting director, it may not be about you. Remember to control only what you can control: your unique choices. So even if in their opinion you are not right for the role, you will be remembered for future projects because you gave such a prepared audition.

6.5 Asked to Prepare Multiple Scenes

If you are auditioning for a large role, the casting director will often give you two different scenes to read in preparation for the audition. Sometimes more. When you think about the fact that they are trying to cast a lead role based on the reading of only a few scenes, a certain strategy of choosing which scenes to read becomes paramount in the audition process. On our side, we want the material to show how wide the actor's range is. We also want to see a different aspect of the character from scene one to scene two. It is the actor's job to understand that this is always the casting director's goal, so in preparing for the audition, approach each scene looking for those differences.

This difference in the two scenes can often trip the actor up in the intellectualizing about it. **Remember that you often can't audition a scene the way you will ultimately perform it when actually filming it.** The sides are lifted out of the context of the full script and stand alone with a beginning, middle, and end. When back in context of the full script, the sides have full scenes bookending them, and the way they will be played and directed could be vastly different when filming.

* * * * * * * * * * * * * * * *

Producers Pen Densham and John Watson hired me to cast the remake of Carrie, *the popular horror film originally starring Sissy Spacek, as a television miniseries. We needed to cast several major roles and only had time to read two or three scenes for each role during the audition process. If you saw the original film, you know that the role of Carrie covers a huge range of emotions, from being tormented by her mother, who locks her in a closet, to being humiliated by all the mean girls at school when she has her first period. She also needs to be sweet and shy when a boy asks her to be his date for the prom but then also demonstrate intense ferocity when she blows the entire high school prom away with her telekinetic powers. The scenes we chose for the auditions reflected that broad range.*

One of the audition scenes we used between Carrie and her mother (played by Patricia Clarkson) was an emotional one in which Carrie tries to get her mother to let her go to the prom. We chose this scene because of the opportunity it gave actresses to show their emotional range. During filming, the director would help guide emotional choices, but in the auditioning of it, with the scene lifted out of context of the script, the actresses needed to make their own unique choices, showing their depth and range.

Another scene we gave actresses auditioning for Carrie was one in which timid Carrie is in the library reading a book on sewing when Tommy, one of the most popular boys in school, asks her to be his date for the prom. We read this scene to reveal the shy, sweet side of the title character in stark contrast to the emotional depth required for the other scene.

* * * * * * * * * * * * * * * * * *

If you have an opportunity to show you can go to a deep emotional level, such as crying, and it is an appropriate emotion for the scene, I say go for it. Then if the director or producers don't want the scene to be that emotional in the playing of it, they can redirect and ask you to pull back. But the good news is you will have already shown that you have emotional chops. Quite possibly your character might need to dig deep in another scene in the script, or potentially you might offer a new perspective on the way that scene should be played.

Often when two different scenes are given, the distinction isn't as obvious as the examples just used for *Carrie*. This is typical in half-hour comedy when the tone of the show is clear and the two scenes can feel very similar. It is then the actor's job to find the more subtle differences involving *relationship* and *intention*. When auditioning for a dramedy, an hour-long show with aspects of both comedy and drama, actors should be aware that they will most likely be given one scene that has more comedic aspects and another that is a bit more serious.

The bottom line is that when given two or more scenes in an audition, it is your job as an actor to search for the different aspects of the character in each scene.

6.6 FIND THE CHANGE IN THE SCENE / STAGE DIRECTIONS

Always remember, the intention changes as the scene goes along, also discussed in **2.3 TOOL #3: INTENTION**.

While the casting director is looking for different aspects of the character in the two different audition scenes, it's up to you, the actor, to also find the change in each individual scene. The writer has written a change in the scene—that's what makes the scene interesting and furthers the action of the story. All too often, an actor will be successful getting the intention at the top of the scene right but fail to see where the intention has changed as the scene unfolds. When this happens, the casting director will interpret the performance as a one-note audition.

Here's a good example of what I'm talking about. Let's assume that at the beginning of the scene the writer has written this description in the stage directions:

```
BEN and LAURA, a couple in their late 30s, are in
their living room in the middle of a tense situa-
tion. Laura has just discovered an email from Ben's
lover.

                         LAURA
                      (screaming)
          What do you mean you don't know?
```

The *place* (living room), *relationship* (lovers), *intention* (Laura's to uncover information; Ben's to block information), and *pre-beat* (the email was just discovered) are pretty clear in the writer's description. Many actors, taking the writer's stage direction literally, will start the scene screaming and follow with different levels of yelling throughout the entire scene. This will most definitely produce a one-note audition.

Let's talk for a moment about the writer's description: "screaming." The writer is attempting to help an actor understand what is going on in the scene and to set the tone of the scene. My advice would be to read the writer's intent and then with a big black marker scratch out the word *screaming*, careful not to take that stage direction so literally. Because all too often the writer doesn't write "Laura stops screaming," and the actor gets caught up feeling obligated to scream the entire scene. Use your experience, your intuition, your common sense to bring what's real to you to the scene, and don't be a slave to "directions."

Let's say at the bottom of the first page of dialogue a change happens in the scene when a new character enters the room:

```
EVAN (5 yrs. old) wanders sleepily into the room
rubbing his eyes.

                        EVAN
     Mom, I woke up. Can I sit in your lap till
     I fall asleep?
```

(*The auditioning actress continues to scream)**

```
                        LAURA
     No Evan, go back to bed!
```

Unfortunately, the new *intention* (soothe/protect) and new *relationship* (mother/son) is not recognized by the actress auditioning for Laura as she continues to follow the writer's original direction of “screaming.” In this case as well, the actor risks delivering a one-note audition.

Let’s say the actress auditioning for Laura crosses out the word “screaming”:

```
BEN and LAURA, a couple in their late 30's, are
in their living room in the middle of a tense
situation. Laura has just discovered an email from
Ben's lover.

                         LAURA
    What do you mean you don't know?
```

Now the actress auditioning for the part of Laura has many different choices about where to start the scene emotionally and can simply focus on the words *tense situation*. When you stop the need to “scream,” the intention at the top of the scene (Laura to uncover information, Ben to block information) presents the actress with many different unique choices: whispering, crying, anger, hurt, shock. And when Evan, her five-year-old son, comes in, she can recognize the change in relationship and intention, and her audition will be filled with several different layers of emotions.

An actor who makes the mistake of taking stage directions verbatim will likely be blocked from making unique choices as well as hindered in recognizing the intention change. Moreover, if the actor feels the need to mime all the descriptions in the stage directions, the audition will be distracting and unfocused. (See **1.4 To Mime or Not to Mime: That Is the Question**).

Remember, you can't audition it the way you will film it.

6.7 The Transition Between Scenes

Keep in mind that when you finish your audition for one scene and make the transition to begin another scene, you are being watched at all times. I want you to consider this transition as part of your audition and remain focused. The new scene will have a new *place*, a new *relationship*, a new *intention*, and a new *pre-beat.* Take your five seconds between scenes to visualize your new surroundings and situation. I call it "the bridge between scenes."

Once again, the chair can help you set the new scene for the viewers. If you sat in the first scene, standing for the second scene can help clarify that a new scene is about to start. Moving the chair to a different position can create a new sense of place. I've even seen chairs become another character if visualized clearly by the actor. Or it can be as simple as shifting your position in the chair as you end one scene and begin another. Basically, the rule should be not to end one scene and begin the second scene in the exact same position.

Avoid completely dropping your focus between the scenes by slipping back into being yourself. Doing deep-breathing exercises between scenes, blowing your nose, or even taking a drink of water will suspend the magic for the viewers. As we watch you walk across the room to put the first scene down, pick up the new scene, and then walk all the way back across the room to start the next scene, you have lost our attention and broken the spell. We start looking at the session sheet to see which actor is next.

I remember the first time I saw a proper scene transition take place. The actor we were auditioning ended his first scene sitting in the chair. When he finished, he simply got up and while walking around the chair internally reminded himself of *place, relationship, intention,* and *pre-beat*. It was fascinating to witness, because by the time the actor got around the chair, he had transitioned mentally into the new scene. We were drawn into watching the new scene even before the first line was spoken.

One set of sides I often use in my audition workshops is for the part of Cash from a series I cast called *One on One*, written by Eunetta Boone and starring Flex Alexander and Kyla Pratt. In our fifth year on the air, Kyla's character was going off to college, so we were adding several new series-regulars to the cast.

In the first audition scene, Cash, a member of the paparazzi in search of celebrity sightings, is bragging to Kyla's character, Breanna, about his successful photo exploits. In the second scene, Cash is talking to Arnaz, played by Robert Ri'chard, boasting that he's such a hotshot photographer that he can get Arnaz into any club in L.A. he wants.

The two scenes aren't that different in tone, the distinguishing factor being the difference in the relationship Cash has with Breanna and the one he has with Arnaz.

I loved watching the inventive ways actors chose to use the chair to help distinguish the two scenes. In the first scene with Breanna, the chair was usually positioned facing forward, and the actors went to town trying any number of things:

- Standing beside the chair and leaning on it with one hand with a bit of sexy braggadocio

- Standing behind the chair and leaning on it with both hands in a casual, cocky way

- Sitting in the chair self-confidently with one hand behind his head and legs crossed

- Strutting in front of the chair

- Visualizing that the chair was holding all his camera equipment

- Standing on the chair and jumping off with the line "I jumped from a tree onto her car"

In the second scene, with Arnaz, the relationship was different. Even though the two scenes were similar, the simple act of changing the position of the chair could clearly distinguish the end of one scene and the beginning of another, which the actors evidenced in a number of ways:

- Turning the chair around and straddling it like a bike.
- Lifting one foot onto the chair seat and leaning into his knee.
- Turning the chair around and propping himself on the back of the chair.
- Sitting on the edge of the chair, leaning forward in an "I've got a secret" kind of way.
- Slumping back in the chair nonchalantly.
- Standing in front of the chair, arms crossed, macho style.

Remember, the casting director wants to see a difference between scene one and scene two: By taking five seconds to transition between scenes; by focusing on a new *place*, new *relationship*, new *intention*, and new *pre-beat*; and by finding creative ways to use the chair, the actor can flawlessly bridge the scenes.

6.8 Starting Over / Mistakes

Starting the scene over is never a great thing, but the timing of when you do this can make a big difference. If you are only a few lines into the audition and you feel "off" or realize you aren't focused, this is the best time to stop the scene and ask if it's okay to start again. Usually the viewers will be fine with that.

You don't want to get halfway through the scene and at that point ask if you can start over; this is pretty annoying on our side of the table. We would prefer that you dig in and regain your focus or pause briefly and go back a few sentences, never breaking character. It's also acceptable to pause and say to your reader, "I'd like to take it from the top of the page," as long as you stay focused.

What you don't want to do if you lose focus or flub your line is drop the character entirely and say, "I'm sorry, can we go back a bit? I've lost my line." Pointing out to us so clearly that you have dropped character makes us nervous that you may not be disciplined or seasoned enough to be on our project.

* * * * * * * * * * * * * * * *

The most incredible example I witnessed of an actress forgetting lines but never breaking character occurred when I was casting a pilot and we were testing at the network. This actress had already been through the pre-read with me, two callbacks for the producers, and a reading at the studio for the executives. It was for a half-hour multicamera comedy, and her character was ditzy, funny, and sexy. She had scored the past four auditions, landing all the jokes on target and leaving us in stitches every time.

As the actress walked into the network audition and I was already in my seat ready to read with her, I gasped to myself as I noticed she was not holding her sides. As discussed in **1.2 MEMORIZATION**, *I advise actors to hold the sides throughout the* *entire audition process, even at the network test. On our side of the table, we would always rather an actor glance down at the sides and quickly grab a line rather than watch them squirm to remember the correct words. Also, walking in without sides in your hand can send the message to the viewers that you are at performance level. And you're not yet at performance level. It is still an audition, and having sides in your hand sends that subtle reminder to the viewers. Having said all that, certainly by the network test, your goal should be to know your lines and not look down at the sides.*

Her audition was going along great with lots of giggles from the network executives, which can be unusual, when all of a sudden I realized this actress had just skipped about a page worth of dialogue. I quickly said a line to her, trying to guide her back on course, and she answered with something that made sense but was not in the script. I found myself improvising with her as best I could, all the while amazed that she was not breaking character... not even a little. She was delivering everything the writer had intended, just completely off course from the scripted dialogue.

I could see out of the corner of my eye that the executives and producers were convulsed with laughter, barely containing themselves, all but falling out of their chairs. This actress was showing us that she was a skilled, first-class improviser, which in half-hour comedy is golden. We didn't doubt for one moment she could learn the lines as written if she got the part; we just had to look at her resume to be assured of that. Since half-hour comedy is being constantly rewritten, even during the taping of the show, we knew we had something special in this actress, who could think fast on her feet. She booked the part.

* * * * * * * * * * * * * * * *

The moral of this tale: If you make a mistake (and you will), make the mistake in character.

6.9 GETTING DIRECTION / CAN I DO THAT AGAIN?

Getting direction is always a good thing. Some actors worry that getting direction means that they did something "wrong." You will never be asked to do the scene again unless the casting director, director, or producer saw something in your audition that they think could be right for the role.

It always amazed me when I would give an actor a direction only to get pushback about why those particular choices were made. If you get even a little bit defensive about getting a direction, you might come off as arrogant or not a team player. Often you are given a direction to see if you can show another emotion or side to the character that may come up elsewhere in the script. Even though you may see no link as to how this direction fits into this scene, try your best to adjust and do what is asked. It's even possible you are being given direction just to see if you can take direction. I'm sure you've been in a situation where they said, "Okay, that was good. Now do the scene again a different way."

Once given a direction, afterward it's fine to ask if that's what they were looking for. And now that you have a dialogue going, it's a great opportunity to discuss what you were going for the first time you did the scene. You never know, it may be possible to do the audition yet again. Show them that you can take their direction first, and then they'll be open to discussing your ideas.

With that said, you always want *them* to take the lead in whether you do the audition scene again. Asking "Can I do that again?" after you have finished your audition is usually a pretty painful request for us to hear on our side of the table. Sometimes we feel bad and let you do it again even if we have already made up our minds that you are not right for the part. Then we are anxious because it puts us behind schedule. And if you aren't a lot better or make the same flub you did the first time around, you have made things worse for yourself.

You definitely don't want to ask, "Can I do that again a different way?" That needs to be at the viewers' discretion. If they say yes and you do the scene again exactly the same way, then you should have quit while you were ahead, because once again, it just tarnishes their opinion of your abilities.

THE AUDITION BIBLE CHECKLIST

DEMYSTIFYING THE AUDITION PROCESS

- ✔ Don't try to figure out what "they" want.
- ✔ Don't ever tell yourself you are wrong for the part.
- ✔ Bring your personality to the part and make it right for you.
- ✔ Don't go to the audition to get the part.
- ✔ You are given two different scenes for the audition because they want to see your range as well as various aspects of the character. Find the differences.
- ✔ Find the intention change in each scene. In longer scenes, there are two or three changes.
- ✔ Be cautious about taking stage directions too literally.
- ✔ Transitions between scenes should be part of the audition. "Bridge" the scenes together by taking your five seconds.
- ✔ When losing focus or a line, it is better to stay in character and glance down at your script to get back on track. Don't drop character if you make a mistake.
- ✔ Getting direction is a good thing. Try to take direction even if you don't agree. You'll show them you can take direction.
- ✔ Don't ever ask, "Can I do that again?"

CHAPTER 7

THE BUSINESS OF ACTING

* * * * * * * * * * * * * * * * *

The first step to a better audition is to give up character and use yourself.

Michael Shurtleff

7.1 WHAT DO YOU DO BEST?

After all your training (the dance classes, voice classes, acting classes, improv classes), you may well feel you're ready to conquer any aspect of show business. And you probably are. But you may be shocked to learn that after all that money spent on classes, you have actually chosen a buy/sell business just like any other. I know the creative genius in you does not want to hear this—the truth hurts sometimes—but the sooner you get a handle on this (and not resent it), the sooner your career will significantly benefit.

Take a look at what your strength is as an actor. Do you find comedy comes naturally to you and comic timing is in your blood? Are you in close touch with your emotions and able to trigger tears easily? Your initial answer will possibly be that you can do both. Maybe. *But what do you do best? How do other people see you? How do you get cast most of the time? Are you a character actor or a leading lady?* You need to figure this out, because in this buy/sell business, you must put your best and strongest foot forward.

In my audition workshops I often use the example of Jim Carrey when discussing "What do you do best?" When Jim Carrey first hit town he was such a comedic genius on *In Living Color* that no one would ever have even thought about casting him in a drama. It was several years later, after he had become a star, that he was able to show us that he indeed was good at drama as well. But he'd entered the playing field with his strength of comedy. Doing what he did best as an actor scored in a big way.

7.2 WHAT PRODUCT ARE YOU SELLING?

Casting directors are often searching for a certain look. Sometimes this takes precedence over who may be the better actor. So when you walk into the audition room, it's possible that we "type you out" just by your physical appearance.

I need you to take a long, hard, objective look in the mirror to assess yourself and determine what product you are selling. You have distinctive qualities and a look that is uniquely you, aka your "brand."

Your brand is all those innate qualities you have and consists of two essentials: *physical look* and *personality*.

<u>Physically are you</u>:

A leading man/woman

A character actor

Personality-wise are you:

The quirky best friend

The never-gets-the-girl type

The catty drama queen

The educated and sophisticated leader

The mean girl

The strong, silent type

The control freak

The goody two-shoes

The geeky sci-fi fan

The sexy, spacey type

The Type A personality

The edgy, mysterious type

The earnest good guy

The arrogant jerk

The scary bad dude

The solid-as-a-rock type

The port in a storm

Once you've done this, identify working actors who represent your specific brand. Digging further, find out what parts they have been previously cast in. IMDb is a perfect tool for discovering this information.

If I find an actor is confused as to what product he's selling, I ask him to determine if he'll play more white-collar roles or blue-collar roles. That said, however, an actor can also play both within his brand.

Take, for instance, Julianna Margulies, star of *The Good Wife* on CBS. She is educated, poised, sophisticated, well-spoken, and certainly believable as a high-powered attorney and wife of the governor. This is a quintessential white-collar role. But previously, Julianna Margulies portrayed a nurse on the long-running NBC series *ER,* a blue-collar role for which she earned an Emmy Award for Outstanding Supporting Actress. She could straddle the two worlds because her specific brand consisted of the physical qualities of a leading lady combined with the personality (strong, solid, and willful) found in both white and blue-collar professions.

There is considerable crossover between the parts that leading actors and character actors can play. For instance, lawyers come in all shapes, ages, sizes, genders, and skin colors. If the writer writes that "the defense lawyer is in his fifties, balding and pudgy," we're being told that a character actor is seen in this part. If the writer indicates that "the defense lawyer is in his fifties, an aggressive Tom Cruise type," it is understood that a leading man is visualized in the role.

Unlike in the theater, where you're able through costumes, makeup, and a far-away audience to transform yourself into whatever you want to be, in television you are dependent on the camera, which is up close and personal and sees you very clearly. If they're casting an edgy mean girl from the 'hood and you have the face of a sweet, freckle-faced innocent, can you act the part? Probably. But as soon as the actor who's cast appears onscreen, we need the audience to "get it" instantaneously. Your fresh-faced innocence will not send that message, so you're unlikely to book the part.

It's very freeing when you as an actor can stop beating yourself up and accept your skin color, height, weight, and age. Only one of these four things listed (weight) could actually change; the others you're stuck with. And these four things are often the reason you get cast or not. So what product you're selling is the first determination you must make, even before you get your headshots taken.

7.3 Your Headshot

The most important tool in your actor's toolbox is your headshot. This might sound obvious, but *it has to look like you!* It's extremely frustrating to a casting director who's called someone in to audition only to find that the person who enters the audition room looks nothing like the person in the headshot. When working with a headshot photographer, be wary of a makeup artist applying more makeup than you would normally wear so the outcome is a glam shot. And please don't allow those fabulous wrinkles you have earned to all be airbrushed out of the picture. When you walk through the audition room door, you should look exactly like your picture so the viewers can immediately identify who you are.

Actors can get a lot of conflicting advice about headshots, often hearing that they need a variety of shots representing any and all parts they may ever be called in for—comedy shot, drama shot, mom shot, sexy shot, nurse, lawyer, drug addict, teacher, CEO, homeless person, and so on. These many different types of headshots are necessary only when auditioning for TV commercials.

The theatrical (film, TV, and theater) actor should aim to find what I call your "go-to" headshot—that one great picture that looks exactly like you and reflects your unique personality... thus selling your brand.

That said, however, it is also a good idea to have one or two additional headshots that suggest more specific roles you can portray within your brand—for instance, your "go-to" headshot, a lawyer/doctor/CEO shot, and a dad/Little League baseball-coach shot.

Now that you have decided what product you're selling, you need to capture that when hiring a photographer and getting your headshots taken. Discuss your casting and the product you're selling with the photographer, who can then advise you on what clothes to bring to the photo shoot. If you've determined that you'll be playing the lawyer, doctor, or CEO, you'll definitely want to bring a jacket or suit to your shoot. You might also have decided that your range includes playing, say, a soccer mom, so you'll want to bring a more casual outfit as well. The frustrating part is that the search for that one good headshot can be elusive. I have found that for actors who are unsure of what product they are selling, that one good headshot will likely remain confoundingly out of reach.

In my audition workshops I send out scenes for class the day before we start, to simulate the usual time frame in which an actor has to prepare; getting the material twenty-four hours ahead of the audition is pretty standard. I make sure the actors have emailed me their pictures and resume so I can assign the right scenes for them to work on in the workshop. I take a long look at their picture and resume and ask myself: *Do they look like their headshots? Do their headshots reflect their brand?* If I am misled by their picture, I may possibly choose scenes for them to work on in class that are not a good fit.

* * * * * * * * * * * * * * * * * *

An actress I had never met signed up for my audition workshop and emailed me her picture and resume, which is the first step to join my class. If I don't already know the actor, that picture and resume is the only tool I have in assigning the right sides to work on.

I looked at her picture for a long beat, because I couldn't get a handle on her age or body type. The headshot was zoomed in tight on her face, showing no shoulders or neck, and she had a very round face that took up the entire 8 x 10 frame. I started to make assumptions based on what was in front of me. I decided that since her face was big and round, her body was probably on the largish size. Her age was really throwing me, because the picture made her look like she could be anywhere from eighteen to thirty-five. But I didn't call the actress to ask, realizing that this would be a perfect teaching moment for the entire audition workshop. If the actress was submitting this picture to casting directors, they would be just as confused as I was, and I wanted the class to understand just how important a tool their headshots were.

I dived in and picked sides that described the character as a thirty-five-year-old woman fifteen pounds overweight who had a young child. The first night of class as the actors gathered in their seats, I searched for the actress with the round face. I couldn't pick her out, and no one came up to me to complain how wrong their sides were. When it was time to do the scenes and I asked who'd been assigned the part of Georgia, this tiny, thin woman beamed at me and said that she had the sides.

She breezed through the scenes, reading the lines that expressed how she needed to lose fifteen pounds without a hint of anything being askew. I still couldn't tell how old she was, but her relationship with her young daughter was so convincing that age didn't matter. Despite the disconnect between who she was and the character she was portraying (a disconnect she in fact had inadvertently engendered), this actress had also brilliantly demonstrated to the whole class one of my most important lessons: ***Bring your own personality to the part and make it right for you.***

Needless to say, I still pointed out her headshot to the class, and they all learned the valuable lesson that if the casting director is confused by your headshot, you probably will never make it into the audition room in the first place. And if you do get called in from a picture that looks nothing like you, chances are you could alienate that casting director, because the person you are, standing right there, is not the person in the headshot the casting director chose. Not good no matter how you look at it.

(By the way, that wonderful actress got great new headshots taken and is now soaring in her acting career.)

* * * * * * * * * * * * * * * *

When you capture your essence in a headshot, you'll be able to submit this one shot for all projects (comedy or drama), because that's the person who will walk into the audition room; you'll be looking entirely like yourself. The product you are selling and your brand will be crystal clear.

7.4 Agent Is the Seller / Casting Director Is the Buyer

FACT: The agent is the seller and the casting director is the buyer.

It might be frustrating for well-trained actors to wrap their head around the fact that they are a product to sell, but that's the reality of the business. When agents meet you for possible representation, they are looking for something beyond just your acting abilities; they are looking for where you might fit into the landscape of what is currently casting out there, what television shows are on the air, or what films are currently gearing up.

Agents and managers want to make sure their client lists have a variety of types to offer, so a balance of leading actors versus offbeat character actors is important. They also don't want to have a lot of conflict between actors they represent. In other words, they wouldn't want to have twenty actors in their stable that they pitch as an "edgy bad guy." And by the way, neither would you.

The horrible truth is that an extremely versatile actor can often be a hard sell. Agents need to be able to grab onto something when pitching you to casting directors. By figuring out what your own strength is as an actor, you will be helping agents and managers know how to sell you and what projects to submit you for. Their job is to get you into the room with casting directors.

Unfortunately, in today's market, it's increasingly challenging for an agent and/or manager to get actors auditions in general, and it's even more difficult when the casting director is not familiar at all with the actor's work. Having a hook such as "She's a cross between Meryl Streep and Scarlett Johansson" or "He's the Australian Brad Pitt," or "He's the next Jonah Hill" quickly gives the casting director a context and a more specific and visceral feel for this unknown actor that can be a vital tool in getting the actor seen. Again, this is a buy/sell business like any other, and you are a product to sell.

If you're searching for an agent, the best agency guide currently out there, *The Actor's Guide to Agents,* is published monthly by Samuel French and has West Coast and East Coast editions. Another monthly agent and casting director guide to look for is *Call Sheet,* published by Backstage. The Samuel French Bookshop in L.A. and the Drama Book Shop in New York are the best places to pick up your copies.

7.5 WHAT SHOWS ARE YOU RIGHT FOR?

Now that you have figured out what product you are selling, you need to watch *everything* on television to see which shows on the air might be buying your product. Again, your generation of actors has incredible resources at your fingertips to funnel instant information. Hulu and other websites like it allow you to watch any episode of any television series on the air.

If you have determined that you enjoy doing comedy but your strength is drama, I would suggest you first target the drama shows on the air. Consulting casting director guidebooks will help you find out exactly who is in charge of casting each show and the office's current address.

Many actors feel stuck if they don't have an agent and wonder what they can do on their own to help advance their career. The answer? Lots. Casting director guidebooks at the Samuel French Bookshop in Los Angeles and the Drama Book Shop in New York are available that list not only the casting directors' current address but also the shows they're currently casting. I like Breakdown Services' *C/D Directory: The Professionals' Casting Directory,* because in the back of the book is a list of all the television shows currently casting as well as which casting office is assigned to the project. You can first find the show you want to target and then locate who is casting it. With that info you can now find the casting director's address, also listed in the book. Another great, online service to help find casting directors is called *CastingAbout.com,* a paid service but really worth it for up-to-date projects being cast for film and television both in Los Angeles and New York.

I suggest you limit the number of shows you're targeting to no more than ten. This way you will be really focusing your energy on shows that you know you could be cast in right now. Rein yourself in from trying to target all the shows on the air, because it will diffuse your time and energy. By educating yourself as to who casts what, you will be building a relationship with casting directors, whether they know it or not.

7.6 POSTCARDS

Postcards are a great way to stay in touch and target casting directors. You will hear a million different opinions about this, some people claiming the things just get tossed into the trashcan, so why bother. My own experience gives me quite a different take on this.

Believe it or not, small parts are often the hardest for a casting director to cast. Agents generally don't want to work on those smaller parts, being more focused on trying to get their actors seen for the lead or guest roles. Those small parts can often make or break a scene, so casting directors always want good actors playing them. The problem is that actors who were once willing to do those smaller parts will not always feel that way. There's quite a turnover of who is willing, and casting directors don't always know those actors.

An advantage to postcards is that they arrive on the casting director's desk and don't have to be opened; they're right there on the desk, all those faces staring back at you. I would often glance through the postcards, and if I found a face that interested me, I would put it in a file to remember for a future project. And some days, yes, I would pick the whole pile up and throw it into the trashcan. Other days in a panic, needing to bring in actors fast for a two-line part, I would shuffle through all the new ones on my desk and grab a handful to call in.

Several casting director friends of mine say they love postcards as great tools to help remind them that you're out there, especially if you don't have an agent submitting you. Postcards are also a way for you to write a quick thank-you note to the casting director or to mention when you have booked something or will be in a project. They are one of the strongest marketing tools you have.

Might they go in the trash? Possibly. But if you don't send them out at all, you could be eliminating the possibility of being in the right place at the right time. Taking concrete action toward your goals and desires is the only way to bring your dreams into creation. You can't just wish it so.

7.7 Your Demo Reel

If you are meeting with an agent in Los Angeles, one of the first questions you'll be asked is, "Do you have a demo reel?" If you have only done theater up to this point, it can be a pretty painful question. Putting a theater performance on a demo reel is not going to fly in Hollywood. Neither is filming a scene from your acting class.

Agents want to see your acting ability and how you look on-camera. This can usually be accomplished only with actual clips from television shows, produced films, or commercials that you have been cast in. If you don't have any clips to put together to make a demo reel, then you might need to bring in a scene or monologue for an agent to view your work.

Casting directors also might ask to see your demo reel if they liked your work in the audition room but want to see how you photograph on-camera. A few companies have sprung up in Los Angeles that will write and film scenes for actors who are in need of a quality demo reel. One company, Create Your Reel, meets with actors to determine how they're likely to be cast and what product they're selling, and then writes specific scenes for the individual actor. Their film quality is excellent and the final product looks like an independent film.

Demo reels can be as short as one minute or as long as five minutes, so once you start to accumulate footage, it's important to get your clips together as soon as possible. This will become one of your most valuable tools.

7.8 Casting Director Workshops

All casting director workshops are not created equal. Many such workshops abound, and you'll need to do some research to weed out the chaff—to determine what the format is, what casting offices attend those workshops, and what the financial commitment is. These workshops can be a very valuable tool if the actor is targeting particular casting offices, or they can be a waste of resources if they're only moneymaking organizations. So beware.

Let's say you now know that your strength is drama, you have weapons training, and you can easily play a bad guy. One of your targeted shows is *CSI,* and you have found that Carol Kritzer of Ulrich/Dawson/Kritzer casts the show. Now's the time to research if anyone from Ulrich/Dawson/Kritzer attends casting director workshops, and if so, which ones. At these workshops the actor may meet with only the associate or assistant from the casting offices, but these people still have the power to bring actors in to meet their bosses.

Attending casting director workshops is often a great way to get introduced to a casting office, and you may have the good fortune to get called in for something specific.

7.9 THE ACTOR IS THE CEO

You are the CEO of your own company. I know you didn't go into this business of acting to be a CEO. You thought that's what agents and managers were for. But understand this well: Even if you have an agent, manager, lawyer, and/or publicist, *all these people work for you, the actor.*

I watched many actors when they first got to Los Angeles or New York decide that their top priority was to get representation. They obsessed over this at the expense of taking acting classes and were not proactively educating themselves as to who was who in the business. And then as soon as they did get representation, they put their career into the hands of the agent and expected to be running around on five auditions a day. As weeks or months went by and their phone never rang, they wondered what went wrong.

They gave up their power, that's what went wrong. By not taking control of their career in the first place, by not jumping into acting classes, networking, and building a community, the actor became dependent on someone else as to whether he worked or not. Educating yourself as to what shows are in production and figuring out who the casting director is on each project is the job of the CEO actor.

If you are in Los Angeles, run to the Samuel French Bookshop and stock up on all the books you can to educate yourself about who's who in town—the casting directors, the agents, the managers, the teachers. Read these as if they were textbooks. Consult as well the many how-to books to help actors with their craft. This is the one-stop store for all things show biz.

If you're living in New York, the Drama Book Shop will be your Mecca. Look for readings and book signings in both stores to hone your networking skills.

Whatever other obligations you have during the course of a day, be sure to carve out time to run your business as CEO actor. I'm not asking you to devote huge chunks of time every day to this; I'm asking you to take an hour or two (preferably in the morning) ignoring the phone, computer, text, and Twitter and do something proactive about your career:

- Watch a show on television that you have never seen. Hulu is great for this.

- Go to the Samuel French Bookshop in Los Angeles or the Drama Book Shop in New York to peruse and network.

- Buy casting director and agency guides and read them like textbooks.

- Make a list of TV shows you are right for.

- Research who the casting director is on each of your targeted shows.

- Ask other actors who their agents and managers are.

- Get on IMDb and find out who the agent is for your favorite actor.

- Write two postcards to casting directors.

- Write a cover letter to an agent.

- Go audit an acting class.

- Research some casting director workshops.

- Ask actors who their photographer is and check out their website to view their work.

- Make a list of any casting directors, directors, producers you've worked with before or have met in an audition. Put them on your contact list when you have reasons to send out postcards. This is building your community.

THE AUDITION BIBLE CHECKLIST

The Business of Acting

- ✔ Determine what it is you do best. What is your strength as an actor?
- ✔ Determine what product you are selling. Lead or character? Blue-collar or white-collar?
- ✔ Make sure your headshot looks like you.
- ✔ Realize that your headshot is your brand.
- ✔ Understand that the agent is the seller and the casting director is the buyer.
- ✔ Draw up a list of shows you know you are right for and target the casting director.
- ✔ Create postcards and send them; they're a great marketing tool.
- ✔ Get a demo reel together; this is becoming increasingly necessary.
- ✔ Consider participating in a casting director workshop, but remember that they are not created equal. Do your homework.
- ✔ Never forget that you are the CEO of your own company.

PART TWO

AUDITIONING FOR A SERIES-REGULAR ROLE

I don't dream at night; I dream all day; I dream for a living.

Steven Spielberg

In the television world, a unique process takes place every year from January to April during what is called *pilot season.* This is when the major networks try out new scripts and material in the hopes of having a hit TV show; they've agreed to finance, shoot, and cast one episode of the show to see if it works or not. This is called the *pilot*.

Over the previous months, studios have hired writers and executive producers to create these new storylines and scripts and then pitch them to the networks. If the networks like the new concept, they will order a pilot to be written. This is called a *pilot pickup.* Casting for these new pilots usually starts mid-January and ends in April.

In mid-May the networks announce their upcoming fall and mid-season TV schedule, usually airing from the following mid-September through mid-May. By the end of April, all the pilots have to be ready to be viewed so the network executives can decide which ones to pick up for series … or not.

The networks need to sell their new product to advertisers. So annually, the third week of May, they hold the *upfronts* in New York, where with much fanfare they present their new shows to advertisers with the hope they will buy commercial time early.

As the landscape of TV has expanded tenfold, with the addition of different cable stations and summer programming, the traditional time period when pilot season takes place has loosened up considerably. Pilot season now can take place year round, with networks developing a new script and casting it whenever they feel it is ready. This is certainly a bit of relief when casting, as during past pilot seasons everyone seemed to be scrambling to grab the same list of actors.

Cable stations (HBO, Showtime, USA, etc.) have a different season for airing their shows from that of the major networks, typically late spring to late summer. This proliferation of TV stations and expanded summer programming has opened up casting of new pilots and series to be more of a year-round business.

Nonetheless, as long as the major networks continue scheduling a new fall season each year and need to sell their product to advertisers, some form of the traditional pilot season format will exist.

I have cast many pilots over the years, and as a Senior Vice President of Casting for The Greenblatt Janollari Studio and Director of Casting for CBS I oversaw the casting of many more. The casting process to add a series-regular role to a pilot or an existing series has been the same all these years:

1. The Pre-Read with the Casting Director
2. The Callback for Producers
3. Reading for Studio Executives
4. Testing at the Network

Yes, some actors will skip the pre-read because they are known to the casting director, and other actors might have a high enough profile to do a one-time-only read for the studio or network executives. But for our purposes, demystifying the steps to casting a series-regular role on television is key to conquering the audition process, and understanding what part of the process you have control over and what part of the process you don't have control over is critical.

It is not your job to worry if you are too old, have the wrong hair color, don't have enough experience, are the wrong skin tone, and so on. It is your job to make unique choices, be prepared, be confident, be consistent, and be mentally focused. To quote one of my students, Seana Kofoed *(Men in Trees)*:

"The four steps of testing are pre-read, producers, studio, and network. I think the more we can arm ourselves with what each step is about, the more at ease we'll feel. It demystifies it, which is exactly what this process needs: brings it down from the epic to the mundane."

Chapter 8

The Pre-Read With The Casting Director

* * * * * * * * * * * * * * * * *

The moment you doubt whether you can fly, you cease forever to be able to do it.

J. M. Barrie

8.1 The Casting Office

The *pre-read* is usually held in the casting director's office. You are usually being auditioned by the casting director first because she either doesn't know your work or has not seen you do this kind of part before. This office is often a small room, and you'll usually see a lot of other actors waiting in the lobby. I always say the lobby of the casting office is your first line of defense. You will see all those other actors and imagine they're just waiting to sabotage you. But really, you must stay mentally focused in the lobby to avoid the pitfalls of self-sabotage.

You notice an actor you recognize across the lobby, you observe what the other actors are wearing, and you hear the casting assistant on the phone checking the availability of a "name" actor for the part you are auditioning for. You say to yourself, *I'm never going to get this part. That actor has a lot more experience than me!*

Make sure you stay focused on your own choices in the lobby, and avoid chitchatting with other actors. Get into the mental focus of the athlete. When your name is called, enter the audition room with *confidence*. This is where the audition starts—from the moment you walk into the room.

Please make sure you do not enter the room in character, but in a hybrid state of being a focused actor ready to go, as well as a pleasant person open to whatever the casting director throws your way. If chitchat happens, make sure that when it is over you take your five seconds to regain your mental focus before you start the scene. Making as much eye contact with the casting director or whoever is reading with you during your audition is key.

I hate the word *memorize*, because actors who try to memorize the scene usually are searching their heads for the right words during the audition instead of thinking of what their *intention* is in the scene. But be familiar with the material. *Know it.* Please remember, we don't audition you to see if you can memorize lines; we audition you to see if you are at all right for the part. We want an actor to come in prepared with unique choices. Hold the sides in your hand in a comfortable way and glance down and grab the line if needed. The best auditions are the ones when the auditors forget the paper is even in the actor's hands.

The casting director has been hired by the producers to find the cast for their pilot, series, or film and is often hassled, tired, and under considerable pressure to hurry up and come up with that cast. So as you walk into the pre-read with the casting director, you may sometimes pick up mixed signals. The casting director may have just gotten off the phone with the Network Casting office saying they don't like their choices so far. The executive producer may have just called to say that they've written new sides and want all the actors to have the new material in the session that starts in half an hour. Understand that the casting director can be pulled in many different directions between the network, studio, producers, and director.

The actor views the casting director as the gatekeeper, and this is indeed the case, but casting directors, being human, can often unwittingly be their own worst enemy by getting caught up in this behind-the-scenes tug of war with the people producing the project. *Believe me when I say that the casting director wants you to be IT, wants you to solve the problem.* So even if you get thrown a hostile glance or feel ignored, stay focused and ready to go.

After the audition is over, DON'T offer excuses as to how horrible the audition was. DON'T ask if you can do it again a different way. DON'T say, "Would you like to give me some direction?" Asking a casting director to give you direction could be a bit of a minefield, depending on the mood of the casting director. The best way to exit the room after an audition is to again make eye contact and say, "Anything else?" That puts the ball in their court to give you direction if they like. Leave with as much confidence as you entered. "Thanks! Bye!" Out the door.

8.2 We Want You to Be the One

A big cause for audition room nerves is that actors often feel they're being judged by the "powers that be" behind the audition room door. Actors are like sponges, and they have a tendency to soak up all the bad energy in the audition room. The truth is, we are pulling for you and would love for you to be the one to solve our problem. *We need you as much as you need us.*

Actors have chosen a career that dishes out constant rejection, and over time auditions can become more stressful than fun. It's imperative, if you are to stay in this business for the long haul, that you remember back to why you entered this business in the first place. Continually rediscovering that sense of fun you had when you first started out is key to long-term audition success.

* * * * * * * * * * * * * * * *

During an especially grueling casting process for a pilot starring Carlos Mencia, I was having a very hard time finding one of the series regulars for the show, a handsome young cop who also needed to be funny. I know this sounds like a simple thing to find, given the thousands of young actors in Hollywood, but as Barbara Miller, the longtime Head of Warner Bros. Television Casting used to say, "God doesn't give with both hands." Meaning that finding handsome actors or beautiful actresses who are also funny and willing to do a half-hour comedy pilot is the hardest thing for a casting director to come up with, because if they have those qualities they are probably already movie stars.

An agent from William Morris I was friendly with who knew I was having difficulty casting this part called to say he had a hunch about someone he'd just met. He said that this young actor had just gotten off a bus from Dallas and showed up in his office through a referral. (I remember joking with the agent when he insisted that this wasn't a figure of speech—the actor had literally taken a bus from Dallas.) He pitched him to me as a "young Tom Cruise" but didn't know anything about his acting skills. Having nothing to lose I said, "Send him over right now."

I had a lobby full of actors and was pretty much deciding as soon as an actor walked into the audition room if he was right or not. I had read the audition scene so many times that I had it memorized and was feeling like the Barbara Miller "God not giving" quote was becoming my reality. I stepped out into the lobby and spotted the "young Tom Cruise" among all the other seasoned actors, and that wide-eyed, isn't-this-fun grin beamed across at me. As I brought him into the audition room I was sending up little prayers to the audition gods, and with a last shot at hope, started to read the sides.

"Okay, okay," I remember thinking, "not bad." For two hours I worked with this young actor, and every time I gave him an adjustment he took it. His natural charm and conversational approach made up for his lack of experience.

I called my producers and asked if I could bring this actor over, telling them he might be worth a look. When we got to the producers' office I don't think I breathed the whole time I was reading with the actor and waiting for their reaction. I remember a long pause and then ... "Let's do that again."

George Eads went on to be one of the original stars in the long-running series CSI. *He booked that Carlos Mencia pilot, and I cast him later in an NBC movie-of-the-week called* The Ultimate Lie. *I continued to call George in for anything I was casting that he was right for, and he consistently delivered in the room. He always gratefully acknowledged that I took the time with a star-struck kid fresh off the bus from Dallas to give him his first break.*

But it was the way George walked into that first audition room that set him on his path to success. He had a confidence and was truthful to who he was as a person, not trying to be someone else. He had fun. I don't remember any angst coming from him when I first went out to get him in that lobby full of seasoned Hollywood actors. What I remember is that the "certain something" coming from George demanded my full attention.

8.3 Don't Be Late

When I ask other casting directors for their list of pet peeves, actors being late for their scheduled appointment time is usually at the top. There is rarely a good excuse for lateness. It always amazed me when an actor would show up half an hour late and say, "I got stuck in traffic."

You mean there is traffic in Los Angeles? Who knew?

In Los Angeles, auditions are often held on studio lots where the casting director has an office. Since 9/11, security to get onto studio lots has been strictly enforced. Actors' names must be on a list at the studio gate, and they must bring a photo ID to get onto the lot. *How does it happen that an actor drives to an appointment but doesn't have a photo ID along?* It happens. There is a rumor that right after 9/11 Nicole Kidman drove up to the Paramount gate for an appointment and was refused entrance because she didn't have a photo ID on her. True or not, the point is made. Bring your photo ID to every audition, no matter where it is.

On the 20th Century Fox lot, actors must park in an area outside the gates. It can be a very long walk to the casting director's office, so planning ahead where exactly you are going is key. Warner Bros., Universal, Sony, Disney … all the big studios have large lots, difficult parking, and the same security rules.

Casting directors expect actors to know all this and plan how long it will take to reach the casting office. From our point of view, we have given the actor an opportunity and expect promptness. Even more, we encourage you to get there early so you can gather your mental focus while waiting in the lobby. Being late also signals that you may show up late to the set if cast. If an actor arrives late to a pre-read, huffing and puffing and sweating, I would usually tell him to take a deep breath and collect himself. If I ended up calling that actor back to producers because I liked his audition and he was also late for the callback, I would warn the producers that this might be a bad habit for this actor.

8.4 Prepared Three Scenes, Now Reading One

You were up all night preparing those three scenes, twelve pages long. You have a 10:00 a.m. audition and have fueled yourself with caffeine and are pumped and on your way to the casting office. As you enter the packed lobby, you sense frustration on the faces of other actors. Just as you're signing in, the casting assistant comes out and says loudly: "Everyone! We are now only reading Scene 1."

The voice in your head: *Whaattt!! I was up all night! This was my chance to get in good with this casting office. Scene 1 is my weakest scene. This is terrible. What a waste of time and energy.*

Your name is called and you walk into the audition room seething with an anger that is written all over your face. You go though the audition on autopilot and leave the room depressed.

Believe it or not, casting directors don't have you prepare a bunch of scenes and then have you do only one merely to torment you. I'm sure that's how it feels. But know that something has happened on their end of the casting process.

It could be that the part got cast since your appointment was given, but they want to read you anyway to see if you might be right for another part. Maybe an offer has already gone out for this part, but the casting office has to always keep up its search in case someone passes. Maybe the casting director has read hundreds of actors and by now can tell immediately if you are right or not. If you aren't right, no sense in taking up time reading three long scenes when there's so much pressure to fill this part. Time is precious. On the flip side, if you are right for the part, you'll likely be asked to read all the other scenes. And the good news is that you will be prepared.

If you encounter this scenario, please don't let this opportunity to be in front of the casting director go to waste. It is still an opportunity to show your work. Put your ego in check and do the job of an actor today. Doing one scene could be all you need for this casting director to discover their new favorite actor.

An option to consider if told you are now only reading one scene is to quickly assess which of the scenes is your strongest. When you enter the audition room, acknowledge you have been told to only read Scene 1 and ask if it is possible to read Scene 2 instead. But only try this if you are confident that the other scene will better showcase your abilities. The casting director may say "no," but often when an actor made this request of me, I was so relieved to be hearing a different scene that I found the actor refreshing and unique. *Nothing ventured, nothing gained* ... but politely, of course.

8.5 No Perfume

Now, this is something many actors never even consider. Think about it for a moment: A casting director sits in a closed-door office reading actors all day. If fifty actors that day all wear a different perfume or cologne, each will leave that lingering scent behind. As the day progresses and the scents mingle, the result can become an overwhelming, nauseating toxic fume.

If there are no windows as well as a closed door, you can well understand why this is at the top of the pet peeves list.

Save your perfume or aftershave for your next date.

8.6 DON'T TOUCH

I once knew a casting director who had a piece of masking tape on the floor and instructed every actor who came in to read for her to never cross that mark.

Every casting director has had at least one experience of an actor crossing way over that line, literal or figurative, to kiss them, slap them, sit in their lap, stroke their face, sit on their desk, hug them, or even pick up items on their desk and move them around.

Please don't do any of these things.

Keep a comfortable distance from the reader, mainly because if you get too close, you will have a hard time being seen. But truthfully, getting too close to the casting director or reader can be uncomfortable for both parties. Relating to the casting director as a fellow actor can backfire big time. The physical interaction can be misconstrued, even if the actor's choice is innocent.

Visualization **(5.1 VISUALIZATION)** is the most important audition tool for you to master when reading with a non-actor. Remember, this is one of the biggest differences between an audition and doing a scene in acting class or filming on the set. You are *not* working with another actor during an audition, and this is not the place to physically interact. Reserve that for when you're working with a fellow actor.

8.7 Should I Be Witty?

Some actors have been told that they need to make a strong first impression while in the audition room and that they should come up with something witty to say so they will be remembered. I promise you that we can smell it a mile away when an actor is trying too hard to make a good impression and has rehearsed a barb to throw our way. As I mentioned in **4.6 Chatting with the Casting Director**, sometimes casting directors will chat with you and sometimes they won't, but always take your cue from them as to whether chatting happens or not. Being yourself is the best and safest option.

Having said that, I'll admit that some actors are just more naturally witty and can think fast on their feet. It is true that when something organic happens in the room and the actor reacts in a swift, witty way, we can lap it up. But it is not something that can be planned; it only works when actors naturally react to a situation and are comfortable in their own skin.

This is not to say that you shouldn't think about how you will say hi when entering the audition room. Just make sure that the "Hi" reflects your personality, professionalism, and confidence all at the same time.

THE AUDITION BIBLE CHECKLIST

The Pre-Read with the Casting Director

- ✔ Avoid self-sabotage while you're waiting in the lobby of the casting office.

- ✔ Stay focused in the lobby and avoid chitchat with other actors.

- ✔ Enter the audition room with confidence.

- ✔ If chatting happens with the casting director, make sure to take your five seconds to regain your mental focus before you start the scene.

- ✔ Be familiar with the material. Know it.

- ✔ Understand that the casting director is pulling for you and would love for you to be the one to solve this casting problem.

- ✔ Don't be late to your audition appointment.

- ✔ Don't get angry if you have prepared multiple scenes and are told you are now reading only one scene. Don't squander the opportunity.

- ✔ Don't wear perfume or cologne to the audition.

- ✔ Don't touch the casting director.

- ✔ Don't try to plan witty things to say. *Be yourself.*

Chapter 9

The Callback for Producers

* * * * * * * * * * * * * * * * *

It's not the will to win that matters. Everyone has that. It's the will to prepare to win that matters.

Paul "Bear" Bryant

9.1 A Callback Story

I thought an actress I called in often (we'll call her Sarah) would be especially right for one of the leads in a pilot I was casting. I always liked her work, but the one issue I had was that she would frequently change her audition from the pre-read with me to the callback for producers. I told Sarah's manager that I would assure her a callback but asked to work with her first to drive the point home that I wanted consistency from pre-read to callback.

My office at the time was on the Paramount lot in one of those lovely trailers. I was casting a few different series for the studio, and even though this pilot wasn't one of them I was allowed to use the office for whatever I was casting. It consisted of three small rooms: one for the waiting area, one for my casting partner, Liz Melcher, and one for my office. I could fit in only a desk, two chairs, and a small bookshelf, so the actor's audition chair was only a few feet away from where I sat.

When Sarah had her pre-read with me, I couldn't have been more pleased. She was natural, charming, funny, and conversational all at the same time. She swore to me that she would be consistent, and off she went, ready for her callback. She had a great look for a leading lady on television, and I was secretly hoping she would book the part.

Five days later, the callback session was held at the producers' office on the Warner Bros. lot, the studio producing this pilot. When I got over to that office, however, there was some concern that it was too small to accommodate four producers, two casting directors, and the actors, and so we moved to a conference room. To call it huge would be an understatement, plus there was no furniture in it, so we brought in folding chairs and a long folding table and set up the camera.

We tried to scale down the size of the room by arranging for the producers to sit at the table, which faced a wall but left enough room for the actor to stand facing them. However, we didn't realize until too late that the actors would also be facing the rest of that cavernous space.

By the time Sarah came in, we were running almost an hour behind schedule. Moving the audition space had set us back, and actors were piling up in the lobby. A party atmosphere started to infiltrate the lobby, and actors were chatting and laughing so loudly I repeatedly had to go out and ask them to quiet down.

I knew I was in trouble by the way Sarah entered the room. "Hi," she boomed, sweeping in and laughing at something someone in the lobby had said. As she started her audition she began using the space as if it were a stage, walking from one side to the next with her gestures and voice getting bigger and louder. By the time she finished her scene, she was so loud that her fellow actors in the lobby applauded. I looked at my producers, who were stunned into silence.

I called Sarah's manager after the auditions and told him to have her call me, and what we eventually discussed covered many of the core tools, audition techniques, and pitfalls of a callback situation that I'll be discussing in this chapter.

9.2 THE LOBBY DANCE

For a multitude of reasons, auditions can often run behind schedule. A producer/callback session should hopefully not be as chaotic as a pre-read session in the casting director's office. After all, callback sessions are often filled with actors the casting director already knows and hasn't had to pre-read. Many well-known actors could be at this producer session, and the casting director strives to organize appointment times so actors don't have to wait too long. But things can get off schedule.

Actors need to be aware of the lobby sabotage and protect themselves from other actors and a common group dynamic. Some actors have an easier time engaging or joking around and then walking into the audition room, especially if the audition is for a comedy. For other actors, this type of lobby situation can throw them off their game and make it hard to get back into focus when their name is called. That's why it's so important to adopt the mental focus of an athlete while in the lobby rather than be drawn into self-sabotage and distractions that might tank your chances.

When I recommend that you be in your bubble (**3.2 THE BUBBLE**), this does not refer only to preparing serious drama material; it's about being a focused actor. As I mentioned earlier, Jerry Seinfeld uses "getting into the bubble" when offstage waiting to go onstage for his stand-up act. Regardless of the tone of the piece, it is in your best interest to adopt the mental focus of an athlete while waiting to go into the audition room.

And on our side of the door, it can be frustrating to hear loud talking coming from the lobby. Even if we are casting a comedy, it is distracting to the actor in the audition room to hear peals of laughter coming through the door.

* * * * * * * * * * * * * * * *

Sarah walked into an audition lobby that was packed and where people were laughing, talking, and exchanging stories. Instead of retreating to a corner to focus, she got caught up in the revelry. When her name was called she was far removed from her task at hand and entered the audition unfocused and a bit spacey.

9.3 THE WAITING GAME

Actors always complain about having to wait long past the appointed audition time. And they're right. Producers would rather keep actors waiting than have to wait for actors themselves. So it's definitely not an equal-opportunity situation.

That said, self-preservation requires an actor to prepare for the inevitability of having to wait. It's very hard to stay focused in your bubble for a long period of time, I know. I would encourage you to take breaks to clear your head: Walk outside (of course telling the casting assistant where you will be) or listen to music on headphones. The temptation to start chatting and laughing with other actors can be a slippery slope to sabotaging your audition.

On another note, it's understandable that you wouldn't want to eat a heavy meal before your audition, but common sense dictates that the body needs energy to keep going, and blood-sugar crashing has tanked many an audition. So stuff some power bars, nuts, or dried fruit in your purse, backpack, pocket, or briefcase; just a bite or two of a power bar can keep up your energy through a long wait. And bringing along water or an energy drink keeps the body hydrated and prevents you from crashing.

* * * * * * * * * * * * * * * *

When I had my conversation with Sarah about what happened to her during her audition, one surprising thing she told me was that her blood sugar had crashed. She had not eaten all day, and there were no water fountains in the lobby or vending machines in sight. After waiting an hour, she was not only running on fumes but literally shaking from a blood-sugar crash.

9.4 DIFFERENT ROOM, MORE PEOPLE

The callback is usually in a different space than the pre-read, most likely in the producers' office on the studio lot where the pilot is being shot. In the callback room will be the executive producers—usually the writer/creator of the show and two or three other writing or nonwriting producers. The director of the pilot may or may not be present at this stage of casting; a big difference between film casting and TV casting is that TV producers, not directors, are usually the ones who choose which actors will test at the studio and network. Directors come and go on a TV series (they could be off directing another show), so they don't always have a vote in casting.

When you walk into this different, larger room with more people in it, make sure you say hello and make eye contact with everyone. Understand that *the producers in the room think you know who they are.* You certainly should have done your homework to know the names of all the producers, what studio is producing the show, which network the show will be on, and whether it is a half-hour or hour show. But the tricky part is that you may know the names but not the faces. The best way for you to handle this is to sweep all eyes in the room equally. Treat it like you are walking into your living room greeting guests; you don't want anyone to feel offended.

Often the casting director is seated between the most important people in the room, usually the executive producers who are the creators of the show. They want the best view of the actors. However, this doesn't always follow, so make sure you don't make eye contact with only those two people sitting next to the casting director just because I said that is normally the case!

Also, make sure you locate the person you'll be reading with. In the pre-read you may have read with the casting associate or assistant, and now the casting director, who you have never met, is conducting the callbacks. It's fine to ask "Who am I reading with?" or "Am I reading with you, Holly?" Take control of the room. *It's your time, it's your three minutes.*

In a callback, actors see the size of the room with more people in it and sometimes feel as if they have a large house to play to. Projecting your voice to the back wall, gesturing and moving around to "fill it" will often cause the producers to feel you are too "theatrical" for television. It's easy to forget the tone of the piece you're auditioning for when confronted with a large room that feels like a stage and having more people in the room who suggest an audience.

Remember, this is television, and in your callback there will often be a camera framing you up close. It is your job to know if you're auditioning for a half-hour multicamera comedy, a single-camera comedy, a dramedy, or an hour drama, as this will determine the tone of the show, but whatever the case, your acting and presentation will have little to do with the size of the room.

Keep in mind that the camera, which has an embedded microphone, is often several feet away from where you are standing and you will not usually be miked. Several producers in the room will also be watching your audition, so if you speak in a voice that's too low, the viewers will have a hard time hearing you—and when the audition is replayed on camera, it might be almost impossible to hear you.

In adjusting to the subtleties of the camera, actors are told to bring things way down. What actors don't always grasp is that there is a difference in TV and film *acting* and TV and film *auditioning*.

When filming, you have a boom or microphone to pick up your voice and a fellow actor standing close by. There is no need to project your voice to be heard, so low-key conversation and subtle movements are picked up by the camera and boom. Not so in auditions.

In TV and film casting sessions, the reader usually sits next to the camera, so when your audition is watched later, your face and eyes can be seen to the best advantage. The reader also sits a comfortable distance from you to help you be as real and natural as possible. Your job is to make sure you project your voice loudly enough to be heard by the viewers and with enough energy so the microphone in the camera picks up your volume clearly. No need to push. It's only about your use of "energy."

How far away is the person you're reading with? Once you determine this, the best way to overcome the size of a large room that has several people in it is to *make the casting person you're reading with your barometer.* The reader will be seated next to the most important people in the room and the camera, and if you simply make sure the reader can hear you, you're good to go.

* * * * * * * * * * * * * * * *

The mistake Sarah made was in adjusting her audition to the size of the room, not the tone of the piece for the camera. She should have paid no attention to the large space and used the reader as her barometer as to how loud to be. She forgot that this was television, not theater. I learned Sarah had been doing a stage play for the previous three months, so she put on her theater hat when she saw the size of the room and went to town.

9.5 BE CONSISTENT

You have been called back for the producers because *the casting director liked what you did in the pre-read!* The biggest mistake actors make in a callback is to change things; they go home and come up with brilliant new ideas to try. But the goal of the callback is to *be consistent.* When you work on your audition at home, work on making sure the lines are second nature to you. Work on strengthening your *intention*, clearly define your *relationship*, and get great visualizations as to *place*. The only way to be consistent in repeating an audition is not to ask yourself **how** you said a line, but remind yourself of what your *intention* is.

After you finish, you may be given direction. Sometimes this is different from what the casting director told you. But don't think the casting director was misled or that you did something wrong. The producers often have something in mind they haven't fully voiced to the casting director, or they may be giving you direction just to see if you can take direction. They will never have you do something again if they don't like you to begin with; they will have you do it again only if they see something in you that's right for the part. Being given direction it is a good thing. Adjust.

* * * * * * * * * * * * * * * *

When I spoke with Sarah afterwards, I realized that she actually had no idea it had gone as badly as it had. She got so caught up in the size of the room that she wasn't listening, forgot there was a camera in the room, anticipated every line, and was so "in her head" that she thought she'd been consistent from the pre-read.

9.6 No Excuses

"The dog ate my sides." "I was sick all night." "My grandmother died." "My agent didn't get me the material." "My cat ran away." "I filmed all night." "I went to the emergency room." "I was in a car accident." "My wife left me."

This may sound harsh, but we really don't care. At most we might say, "Oh, I'm sorry. Are you ready to read?" If you really feel that whatever has happened in your personal life will interfere with your audition, that you will not be able to get into the mental focus of an athlete for the three minutes you will be in the audition room, then try to reschedule or cancel. You or your agent have worked hard to get you this audition, but unfortunately casting directors, producers, and directors don't forget bad auditions easily. Getting in front of decision-makers when you are not ready will cost you in the long run. It's better to try to reschedule or wait until next time.

* * * * * * * * * * * * * * * *

*In **1.3 What Should I Wear To The Audition?**, I told the story of an up-and-coming young actor who auditioned for the part of a law assistant dressed in torn jeans, a white undershirt, and flip-flops. Believe it or not, this was not the worst part of his time in the audition room. Beyond the fact that he couldn't bother to dress for the audition or that he walked in with an arrogant shuffle or even that he told us he hadn't had time to look at the material, the capper was the bizarre tale he told us next that will forever top my list of most awesome audition excuse stories in the history of audition excuse stories.*

After he told us he hadn't had time to look at the material, he giggled and started telling us a convoluted tale about an audition he had gone to the day before. He said that when he was sitting in the lobby at the other audition, he told the actress sitting next to him that he hadn't looked at the material. She replied that she hadn't looked at the material either because she had had surgery the day before. A lightbulb went off in his head.

He prattled on to us that when he went into the audition room he decided to tell the producers that he hadn't looked at the material because he had had surgery the day before. One of the producers said, "Oh, what kind of surgery did you have?" Not having thought that far ahead, the actor paused and said, "I had my liver taken out." Pause. Pause. The producer said, "You can't live without your liver." Pause. "Oh, did I say liver? I meant kidney," said the actor.

Unwittingly, this actor revealed to us he was a liar.

The actor's agent tried several times to get him back into the room when we were having trouble casting the part. But my producers just couldn't see their way to giving him another shot—not only because he didn't care enough about their project to dress for the audition, and not really because he hadn't bothered to prepare. It was that they would never be able to trust him on the set.

9.7 Don't Change Clothes

Remember, consistency is key in the callback, and that includes showing up in the same outfit you wore to the pre-read or previous audition. I've seen a number of actors lose the part by changing what they were wearing; as good as they were, they didn't "feel" like the character anymore. Keep in mind that the producers have already started to visualize you in the role and also as part of the "world" of the project. So in order to keep that illusion going, make sure you hang on to that outfit.

Many of you may have heard the story Michael Shurtleff tells in his book *Audition* about the girl in the red sweater. It goes something like this:

Michael brought in an actress to read for the director, who loved her. He told Michael to be sure to bring back the actress in the red sweater. When the callbacks came, they got to the end of the session and the director turned to Michael and said, "Where was the girl in the red sweater, you didn't bring her back?" Michael responded, "Yes, she was here today. She was wearing a blue shirt." The director insisted, "No that wasn't her. You didn't bring back the girl I think is the one for the part." The director had started to visualize the actress wearing the red sweater in the role, and when she switched to a blue shirt, he didn't even recognize her.

* * * * * * * * * * * * * * * *

In my years as a casting director I have had similar experiences, the most notable of which was when I brought an actor to the studio to test for a series-regular role for the part of a law assistant. He was a lovely actor, but his look was a bit "off" from what the producers were envisioning. They thought the actor in the role should have a more classic leading-man look, and this actor was just off-center from that. But they liked him enough that they wanted to bring him to the studio executives to hear their thoughts.

The night before we were going to the studio, we had a work session with the five actors we were taking in to read the next day. I told each of the actors to wear the same thing he had on now to the studio the next day, black slacks and collared shirt. I remember one of my producers was standing next to me when I said this, and one of the actors laughingly said, "Wait till you see what I'm gonna wear to the studio tomorrow!" We all laughed, thinking he was making a joke about repeating the same outfit.

The next morning at the Warner Bros. studio, I was waiting in the lobby for the five actors to arrive and glanced up through the glass front-door entrance. Backlit by the sun, I saw a man walk into the lobby wearing a beautiful white suit with a dark red shirt. The swagger was distinctive as this man approached me with a beautiful wide grin.

I realized this man was headed straight for me. As I blinked through the glare of the sun, I realized it was one of my actors—the one from the night before who had joked about wearing something else to the studio! I stuttered through "I thought I told you to wear the same outfit!" and heard him say meekly, "I told you I was going to wear something else."

As my producers gathered in the lobby and saw that this actor looked like he was going on a cruise, they now couldn't visualize him in the world of a law office anymore. I told him to take off the jacket, but there was still the red shirt and white pants to look past. All of a sudden, this lovely actor who was just a bit "off" for the part became an actor in a totally different show! He read for the studio executives, who all agreed he was a nice actor but not right for this part. When this actor chose to wear his best suit to the studio instead of what was right for the character, the magic disappeared.

* * * * * * * * * * * * * * * *

Producers, directors, casting directors, and studio and network executives need to visualize the actor in the part and see if they fit into the world of the show. As unbelievable as it sounds, if the actor changes clothes during the audition process, the viewers' imaginations have to work overtime to see the whole picture. Help yourself and your viewers by choosing clothing that gives a suggestion of the character, and wear the same outfit throughout the entire audition process, unless told otherwise.

9.8 Don't Use a Producer as Another Character

During a producer session, the casting director usually sits in the middle spot, and the most important people in the room flank her on both sides. Sometimes there will be only a few people in the room, and other times there will be many; it solely depends on how many decision-makers are involved in the project. By placing the casting director or reader in the middle, the goal is for everyone to have a good view of the actor during the audition.

Keep in mind that the viewers want to be just that … *spectators*. They don't want to be drawn into the action. The "fourth wall" concept used in the theater should apply to every audition. You would never (well, usually never) speak to individual audience members when you're onstage, so don't ever use one of the producers or the director as a character in the audition scene.

The auditors like to look at your picture and resume, take notes, or possibly whisper to one another during the audition. So give them the space to do their job and for you to do yours.

Whoever is reading with you is there for you to make eye contact with and use as all the different characters you're relating to in the scene. Be sure to use **TOOL #2: RELATIONSHIP** and apply specific visualizations for all the different characters either onto the reader's face or by choosing a thin-air eyeline. The trick when placing a new character into thin air is to have the eyeline be right above the auditors' heads. If you engage the producers eye-to-eye as a character in the scene, they may well feel uncomfortable or annoyed and more than likely be distracted from your audition itself.

* * * * * * * * * * * * * * * *

Once when I was holding a producer session for a pilot, one of the scenes we were reading was between two college students who had run into each other after a one-night stand. I brought in an actor I was really excited about and thought he might book it.

I was sitting in the middle of the couch between one of my male and female producers. The actor walked in looking fantastic and sexy. When he started the scene he was making eye contact with me, using me as the girl. The audition was going great, but somewhere halfway through the scene the actor shifted his gaze to my female producer and started using her as the girl. He inched closer and closer to her sitting on the couch ... as she sank deeper and deeper into the cushions. He ended the scene practically on top of her. There was nervous laughter all around, and the actor left the room.

My female producer was deeply offended that an actor might think that flirting so blatantly with her would win him the role. I personally think it was a spur-of-the-moment decision on the actor's part, but our producer was close to having Security make sure that he had left the lot. To this day I think that actor believes what he did during his audition was a cool move, and I wonder if he ever tried it again.

9.9 There Is a Camera in the Room

There are two circumstances in which you will have a camera in the audition room:

1. You will be going "on tape for producers," so the casting director will record your audition on-camera and send it to the director and producers for viewing.

2. The producers will be "live" in the room, with the camera there as a fly on the wall. Your recorded audition will be watched only if they liked you enough to see how you look on-camera.

More and more casting directors are recording actors' auditions on-camera and sending them off to the director and producers. Many productions are shooting away from Los Angeles now, and technology has advanced to the point where your audition can be viewed within moments wherever in the world the production happens to be shooting.

If your agent tells you that you have an audition and it is on tape for producers, you will be going to the casting director's office to record your audition on-camera. It will most likely be just you, a reader (either the casting director or a casting associate), and maybe someone running the camera. (I remember times when I had to read with the actor and run the camera at the same time.) So expect to be framed tight and not move much.

You will *slate* your name and then do your scenes. More than likely you can ask that the camera be paused between the different scenes so that you have time to adjust. The casting director wants to be sure to send out the best recording possible, so this can actually be a more comfortable audition situation, in which you are collaborating for the best take possible. Always ask how tight you are being framed and let whoever's running camera know if you plan to sit or stand during a scene so the operator will know to follow you. The casting director may offer an opinion about how much movement there can be or limit you to not go past a piece of tape on the floor.

Having a camera in the room during a producer/callback session is almost a given in today's audition world, but in this case the camera functions more like a fly on the wall, recording the entire day of auditions so producers can review them at the end of the day to jog their memory. In this situation you do not need to slate your name or necessarily play to the camera, though it is in your best interest to be aware of where the camera is so you can cheat toward it. If producers are there in the audition room, you will have more freedom of movement and need not discuss your plans to sit or stand in advance. But it's more likely your audition will be a one-shot situation, unlike going on tape for producers, where the casting director may do multiple takes.

As stated in **9.4 DIFFERENT ROOM, MORE PEOPLE**, if there is a camera in the room, it will be a digital camera with the microphone embedded in the camera. This is not the same thing as a film camera, which is used during actual filming. If your volume is too low, the microphone in the camera may fail to adequately pick up the sound of your voice and instead be overwhelmed by the voice of the reader, who'll be sitting closer to the camera.

Understand that you need to project enough so that the microphone in the camera will pick up your voice. It comes down simply to energy. Don't worry; you won't be overacting ... unless, of course, you forget the tone of the piece and start playing to the room as if you were in a theater. It's all about getting the right balance.

Remember, *auditioning* for the camera is different from *acting* for the camera.

* * * * * * * * * * * * * * * *

When I was Head of Casting at The Greenblatt Janollari Studio, at one point we had five series on the air at once. All the casting directors who were casting our shows put guest star and co-star parts on-camera for us so we could see their choices and give approval. Every single one of our casting directors used a camera with an embedded microphone to record the auditions, fluorescent lighting overhead, and a background that was either a plain white wall or filled with messy bookshelves.

I still laugh as I remember Bob Greenblatt and David Janollari telling me to please buy all our casting directors lights and microphones. Besides having a hard time hearing the auditions, they noticed that the shadows thrown on actors' faces from the horrible overhead fluorescents made for vicious circles under everyone's eyes, and it looked like every actor in Hollywood had bad teeth!

In short order I made sure all our casting directors were supplied with lighting equipment and standing mikes. And I must say, actors were approved faster.

* * * * * * * * * * * * * * * *

Most of the time you are going to need to save yourself when going on-camera for an audition. Conditions will often be less than stellar. Wear solid-color shirts that complement your skin tone. Stripes, checks, and designs can be too busy and distract from your face. Also, ladies, you have to glam up a bit for the camera. This is television, after all. A little more eyeliner, a little more lip color will help you pop.

And while we're on this subject … ladies, please watch the "one-eyed" audition. Sexy bangs covering one eye result in an extremely frustrating experience for the viewer; we spend the entire time watching the audition trying to push the hair out of your eyes!

Lastly, I want to mention that self-taping for projects is more common in today's audition world. The casting director may ask an actor to self-tape if they aren't familiar with the actor's work or if the actor lives far from where the project is casting.

All you need is a decent camera (or even a smartphone), a tripod, a few good lights, and a solid colored wall as a background. Recruit a good reader and make sure you frame yourself close, just below the shoulders. When you slate your name, it's a good idea to get a long shot of yourself so they can see your full body.

Being prepared, knowledgeable, and comfortable when there is a camera in the room is the most important audition skill the professional actor must perfect.

THE AUDITION BIBLE CHECKLIST

The Callback for Producers

- ✔ Avoid the group dynamic of the lobby. Stay mentally focused.

- ✔ Be prepared to wait past your audition time due to unexpected delays. Bring water and something to munch on to maintain your energy.

- ✔ The casting director liked your pre-read enough to call you back, so be consistent in your performance at the callback.

- ✔ We don't want to hear excuses, justified or unjustified. If something has happened in your personal life that prevents you from focusing for three minutes in the audition room, then cancel or reschedule rather than risk a bad performance that will disqualify you from consideration in the future.

- ✔ We have started to visualize you in the part, and a major part of that visualization is what you are wearing. Don't change clothes for the callback unless you are specifically told to return in something different.

- ✔ Resist the temptation to adjust your performance to the size of the room the audition is held in. Make wherever the reader is sitting be your barometer as to how loud you need to be.

- ✔ Know the *tone* of the script you are auditioning for. *Tone* has nothing to do with the size of the room you have your audition in.

- ✔ Don't be misled into feeling that because several people are in the room you are playing to an audience. If you do, you will come across as too theatrical.

- ✔ The producers want to be spectators, not actors in your audition. Don't use them as characters in your scene. It may well cause discomfort that will ultimately detract from your audition.

- ✔ If you are "going on tape for producers," you will be able to work more closely with the casting director to get the perfect take, but there will also be less freedom of movement due to the camera's proximity to you. Conversely, when auditioning "live" for producers, you will have more freedom of movement but might get only one shot at the performance itself.

- ✔ Auditioning for the camera is different from acting for the camera.

- ✔ Help yourself when going on-camera by wearing solid colors that complement your skin tone.

- ✔ Ladies, make sure you wear a little more makeup that will help you pop on-camera.

- ✔ Self-taping for projects is more common, so make sure you prepare at home for this posibility.

Chapter 10

Reading for Studio Executives

* * * * * * * * * * * * * * * *

The best advice to fellow actors is this: Know what your job is ... I realized I was going into auditions to get a job. And that simply wasn't what I was supposed to be doing... You're not going there to get a job. You are going there to present what you do. You act. And there it is. And walk away. And there's power in that and there's confidence in that ... The decision about who might get a job is so out of your control that to analyze it makes no sense.

Bryan Cranston

10.1 What Are Your Quotes?

When the producers decide that they want you to read for the executives at the studio who are producing the pilot or series, you first have to make a *test option deal* before you are allowed to read for them. This means that a money deal needs to be put in place for you in case you book the job, and that's because the studio wants to know how much you will cost before they "buy" you. But keep in mind that the "option" in a *test option deal* is always on the studio's side as to whether they will pick up the actor's deal or not. It's not the actor's option to later say he doesn't want to do the show. It's a one-sided deal once the contract is signed.

The casting director calls your agent for your *quotes*. Your quotes are the amount of money you have earned for individual acting jobs. When negotiating a test option deal, the only quotes that really apply are if you have booked or tested for a pilot or series before. If you have never tested before, the negotiators will consider that you have "no quotes."

That certainly doesn't stop your agents or managers from giving out your past money quotes for film, theater, or commercials to help build up your cachet and to start selling how much they think you are worth.

10.2 First You Make a Deal

The business affairs lawyers at the studio will be making your deal with your agent, manager, or lawyer. Technically, a manager is not allowed to negotiate, so if you only have a manager you will need to bring on a theatrical attorney or agent to close the deal. This person will have to structure a contract that includes your pilot fee, your episodic fee if picked up for series, and what *bumps* (increases in money) you get in salary each year over probably a five to seven year period. Sometimes the size of your trailer, the number of loop days included, and merchandising (in case they want to turn your character into an action figure) will also be negotiated here.

The studio already has a budget in place for the entire cast of the pilot, and with the help of the casting director loosely determines how much money is allocated for each part. Of course if there is a lead role in the pilot that may attract a star or someone with name value, more money will be put toward that particular role.

The amount of money that the production has budgeted for the specific part you are testing for could be a bit fluid. That's why getting an actor's quotes is so important. Your quotes can determine if they can afford you, not afford you, or save money on you. And it is your agent's job to get as much money for you as possible regardless of your quotes–short of losing the job for you, of course.

This process can be very contentious, to say the least, so it is in the actor's best interest to let the negotiators do their job. Believe me, if your representatives are good at what they do, they will never recount all the tension-filled phone calls they have with the studio negotiators. "Tension-filled" can actually be an understatement describing this process. But before your deal can be closed, you must agree to it.

Your representatives will walk you through where your deal closed for the pilot and episodic fee. They will let you know how hard they tried to get you more money and hopefully will spare you the details.

During this negotiating process, the actor should concentrate on the job at hand: staying focused on being consistent in the next audition.

10.3 The Work Session

At this point you will have had your callback for the producers, but you still probably haven't had a chance to work with the director or executive producers on a one-on-one basis. If time permits before your studio appointment, you will have about a twenty-minute *work session* with the director, executive producers, and casting director to set a few things and get some direction.

It's possible this could be the first time you meet the director. As mentioned earlier, directors in television are not often attached to just one television series but freelance on multiple productions. It's really helpful if the director can be there for the studio read, so everyone gets on the same page before presenting to the studio executives.

Understand that the executive producers, who are again the writer/creators of the show, want to present the best possible material to the studio executives. Yes, they have already sold their pilot, but it's not over till it's over, so to speak. It is not uncommon at this point for the executive producers to decide to rewrite your audition material and "pump things up" for the studio executives.

This, understandably, can throw actors who have been working on the same material for two, three, or more auditions. But it does happen, and actors need to adjust and not freak out. I always assure actors if and when this occurs that they already have determined who their character is, have strong visualizations for each *relationship*, know where physically the show is located (the *sense of place*), and have an overall *intention* of what their character wants. So they need only treat this new dialogue as having a different conversation.

Rewriting material in television happens all the time, even multiple times a day. Professional actors working in television understand that it should be part of their skill set to adjust quickly to new material.

10.4 THE STUDIO LOBBY

The day of your scheduled appointment to test at the studio, you will more than likely be going to the actual studio lot that is producing the pilot—that means Warner Bros., Universal, Sony, Paramount, Disney, DreamWorks, 20th Century Fox, and so on.

You will see in the studio lobby the other actors who are testing for your part, usually five or six of them and possibly some more who are reading for other parts in the same project. All actors will be given the same appointment time for the audition. So if three different parts are being tested for your project, it's possible that fifteen or more actors will all show up in the lobby at the same time.

I mentioned before that in the testing process for a series-regular role, it is all about the time that the studio executives have to devote to this particular project; the schedule is timed around the executives' schedule, and actors must fall in line and plan to wait. If your audition time is for, say, 3:00 p.m., you'll have to plan to get there at least at 2:30, to get settled in and allow for time to sign your contract. Then plan to wait.

Get into your bubble of focus and touch base with Tools #1-4.

10.5 Signing the Contract

It's not uncommon to have you sign your test option deal right there in the lobby of the studio. Again, be sure to arrive early so you can read it over and make sure it is correct.

It's a good idea to call your agent or representatives before driving to the studio for your audition to see if your contract has closed. This way you can get the news as to what your deal actually is. If your deal has not closed yet, drive to your appointment in any case so that you are on time. But you might have to wait in the lobby, checking in with your agent frequently to see where things stand.

This can be a very nerve-wracking time for the actor and the casting director, because the actor is not allowed to read for the studio executives until the deal is closed. Hearing that auditions are starting but that you cannot go in yet to read can prompt some of the most sabotaging mind games an actor can ever experience. And it's no fun for the casting director either.

The best-case scenario is that your deal has closed and the casting director has four copies of your contract in an envelope for you to sign, right there on the spot. Every actor in the lobby will be given the same envelopes with contracts to sign. If you're smart, you'll get into your own corner and not look over your shoulder at anyone else's contract. You will be very disappointed to see that another actor reading for the same part might be making more money than you. The fact is his quotes were higher than yours, and the producers liked him enough to make his deal and give him a shot at the role. This does not mean this actor will get the part. But if you focus on the discrepancy of money, you will psych yourself out and disrupt your mental focus. Best to get into a corner and pull out the contract that could be as long as twenty pages. I want you to focus on only the first few pages of the contract and trust that your representatives have looked over what is mostly an industry standard agreement, with no hidden agendas.

I have provided an excerpt from a sample contract below and bolded the two things you need to make sure are correct:

1. Your salary for the pilot in paragraph 3
2. Your episodic rate if picked up for series in paragraph 5a Episodic Compensation

ABCD Studios LLC
1000 Hollywood City Plaza
Hollywood, California

Re: Un-Named Pilot/ Role Of "Richard"

Ladies/Gentlemen:

The following sets forth the agreement ("Agreement") reached between **John Doe ("Artist")** and **ABCD Studios LLC ("Studio")**, concerning Artist's services in the role of "Richard" in connection with the above-referenced 60-minute pilot and series ("Pilot" and "Series").

1. TEST DATE: Approximately: March 15, 20XX.

2. PILOT OPTION DATE:

Studio shall have the exclusive option to employ Artist on a pay-or-play basis (pursuant to Paragraph 2 of the Standard Terms and Conditions attached hereto) for the Pilot (the "Pilot Option"), which Pilot Option is exercisable only by written notice from Studio's Business Affairs Department not later than ten (10) business days after the aforesaid test. In the event that Studio exercises the Pilot Option, notwithstanding anything to the contrary contained herein, all of Studio's obligations hereunder, and all of Artist's obligations in the Pilot and/or Series, are subject to Studio's successful conclusion of a license fee negotiation with the licensee; provided, however, if Studio exercises the Pilot Option in writing, and if Studio has not successfully concluded a license fee negotiation with the licensee by May 1st and if Studio has not notified Artist by May 1st that Artist is released from all obligations to Studio because Studio has failed to conclude a license fee negotiation with the licensee, then Studio's obligations to Artist will be fully binding notwithstanding any failure of Studio to conclude a license agreement with the licensee. Notwithstanding the foregoing, once Studio requires Artist to commence rendering services in the Pilot and/or Series, Studio may not thereafter be excused from its obligations on the grounds that Studio has not concluded a license fee negotiation with the licensee.

3. PILOT:

The start date is to be determined. **Studio will pay Artist $XX,000 pay-or-play** (pursuant to Paragraph 2 of the Standard Terms and Conditions attached hereto), for all services in connection with 20 consecutive work days ("Guaranteed Period") (Guaranteed Period includes all compensation and premium pay that may be required for work on a holiday and/or a sixth and seventh day per week). Work days in excess of the Guaranteed Period are payable pro-rata at $/day. Studio shall also be entitled, without additional compensation, to all required additional days for travel, rehearsal and wardrobe, and up to two (2) non-consecutive days for looping, added scenes and retakes (provided, however, that any such post-production services that are not consecutive with principal photography on the Pilot shall be subject to Artist's prior conflicting professional contractual commitments). If Artist's compensation qualifies Artist as a Schedule F Player, Studio shall be entitled to any and all benefits therefrom (except as otherwise expressly provided herein).

4. SERIES OPTION(S):

Provided Studio has exercised the Pilot Option, Studio shall have exclusive, successive, dependent annual options for Six (6) Series years if a fall season start (or Six and one-half (6-1/2) Series years if a mid-season start) to engage Artist's services in the Series. First Series Year option is exercisable only by written notice to Artist given on or before June 30, 20XX. Studio shall have the option to extend its First Series Year option to December 31, 20XX by written notice to Artist on or before June 30, 20XX, followed by a payment in the amount of $XX,000 within ten (10) business days of Studio's notice of its exercise of such option. Subsequent annual options are exercisable only by written notice to Artist given on or before June 30 of the preceding Series broadcast year; provided, if the Series premiere is telecast late midseason (i.e., on or after April 15, 20XX), the Studio may extend the option period for the Second Contract Year from June 30, 20XX through September 30, 20XX by written notice to Artist no later than June 30, 20XX and payment in an amount equal to 1 episodic fee at the last episodic rate paid to Artist, which shall be nonrecoupable against Artist's Second Contract Year Guarantee and shall be paid no later than 10 business days following the date of such written notice. For each Series Year for which Studio exercises its option for Artist's services hereunder, Artist shall be engaged on a pay-or-play basis (pursuant to Paragraph 2 of the Standard Terms and Conditions attached hereto) for the applicable number of episodes guaranteed pursuant to Paragraph 5(b) below.

5. SERIES:

a) EPISODIC COMPENSATION:

First Series Year: **$XX,000 per 60 minute episode** (comprised of $XX,000 and the fee set forth in paragraph 5(c) below).

Thereafter, annual increases equal to five percent (5%) cumulative; provided, however, in the event of a Midseason start in the first year, the increase for the second year will not commence until the production of the twenty-third episode of the Series (including the Pilot in determining the twenty-third episode).

b) GUARANTEE:

i) First Series Year: all shows produced, but not fewer than seven (7) (including Pilot), reducible to six (6) (including the Pilot) if the initial order is for six (6) or fewer episodes (including the Pilot). However, Studio may terminate Artist's employment following completion of the initial order, exercisable in writing not later than the later of:

Ten (10) business days following completion of principal photography of the last episode produced pursuant to the initial order, or (b) ten (10) business days following Studio's receipt of the order for additional episodes. Furthermore, in the event of a Fall start, said termination right shall not expire earlier than December 31 of the first broadcast year. Notwithstanding the foregoing, if Studio requires Artist to commence services hereunder on any additional Series episodes produced beyond the initial order, Studio shall be deemed to have waived the aforementioned termination right.

ii) Second and Subsequent Years: All shows produced, but no fewer than thirteen (13), except that in the event of a first year Midseason start, the guarantee for the second year will be all shows produced, but not fewer than seven (7).

ENTIRE AGREEMENT:

This Agreement between Artist and Studio, including the attached Rider, Appendix I (Standard Terms and Conditions), and Rider to Appendix I, constitutes the entire agreement between the parties with respect to the subject matter hereof. The parties have not relied on any oral and/or written statements that are not included in this Agreement, with any and all such previous understandings having been merged herein. Any modifications to this Agreement must be in writing and must be signed by the parties.

Kindly confirm your acceptance of the foregoing by signing in the space provided below.

Sincerely,

ABCD STUDIOS LLC

By: ____

Signature

____

Type or Print Name

Its: ____

Title

Dated: __________________________

ACCEPTED AND AGREED TO:

ARTIST

______________________________ **John Doe**

Dated: ____________________

If either the pilot money or episodic money are different from what your agent told you, you'll have to stop and call your agent and tell the casting director that there is a discrepancy from what you understood your deal to be. Then the casting director will call business affairs at the studio and get to the bottom of the issue. I have usually found that while the assistant in the business affairs office was typing the contract, your agent finagled another $1,000 out of them and it didn't get translated. At least I always like to think that was the reason.

You will then hand all four signed copies of the contract back to the casting director and get into a corner and focus.

10.6 The Money Sabotage

Having to sign a contract with the dollar signs right there staring you in the face can lead to big dreams for the actor. I have talked to many actors over the years who knew they blew it in their read for the studio because after having signed the contract they walked into the audition room thinking, *If I get this job, I can buy that car!* They did the math in their heads: *22 episodes x $10,000 an episode = $220,000!*

It is imperative to keep your mental focus on the scene … not the money. The way to save yourself from these "voices in your head" is to get back into your bubble and back to the basics of auditioning (your job as an actor).

Adopting the mental focus of an athlete will save you every time.

10.7 Auditioning at the Studio

You will probably have your audition in the casting office of the Head of Casting for the studio. There will be a couch or two, a desk, and several chairs to accommodate all the studio executives attending the audition. It's possible you could have fifteen or so people in the room.

For sure you can expect the President of the Studio for Television Programming, the Senior Vice President of Casting, the VPs of Comedy or Drama Development, and other members of the studio casting department—plus all your executive producers, your director, and the casting director. It can seem like quite the audience. There is generally no chitchat when you walk into the studio read; it's just hi, read, bye. Make sure you take a moment when in the room to locate who you will be reading with. Even if you have read with the same casting director or reader at every audition, you might be reading with someone new at the studio. Take control, making it your space, not theirs, and take your five seconds to focus yourself before starting. Touch base with **Tool #1: Sense of Place, Tool #2: Relationship, Tool #3: Intention,** and **Tool #4: Pre-Beat**. Look at the reader and begin, keeping in mind that your character is in the middle of something.

Ground yourself in the listening using **Tool #5: Listen**. Listening to the words of the reader will flow seamlessly into applying **Tool #6: Respond in the Listening**, allowing you to be present and in the moment.

Take a few moments to transition out of the scene, just as you took a few moments to dive into it. Exit the room with confidence making sweeping eye contact with everyone in the room.

Once you leave the audition room, make sure you don't exit the building until you are told you can leave. It's possible you could be "mixed and matched" with other actors reading for other parts.

It is at this point that the studio executives and the executive producers decide if they want to take the final step of testing you at the network.

THE AUDITION BIBLE CHECKLIST
Reading for Studio Executives

- ✔ You will need to make a test option deal before you read for the studio executives.

- ✔ During this process let your representatives do their job and you do yours. Stay focused.

- ✔ You will hopefully have a work session with the director and executive producers to set some things and get notes.

- ✔ It's possible that several different roles will be auditioning at the same time, so prepare to wait.

- ✔ Be prepared to sign your test option deal at the studio.

- ✔ Check to make sure your pilot fee and your episodic fee are what your agent confirmed your deal closed at. If not, tell the casting director and call your agent.

- ✔ After you sign your contract, get back into the mental focus of an athlete and kick the sabotaging thoughts of money out of the "voices in your head."

- ✔ You will have the studio executives, your producers, the director, and the casting director in the room.

- ✔ Take your five seconds to touch base with: **Tool #1: Sense of Place, Tool #2: Relationship, Tool #3: Intention, Tool #4: Pre-Beat, Tool #4: Listen**, and **Tool #5: Respond in the Listening.**

Chapter 11

Testing at the Network

* * * * * * * * * * * * * * * * * *

Obstacles are those frightful things you see when you take your eyes off your goal.

Henry Ford

11.1 The Lobby, the Room, the People

The last and final step in auditioning for a series-regular role on television is to *test* for the executives at the network. You will be going to the network (e.g., CBS, ABC, NBC, FOX, HBO, Showtime, CW, USA) that has bought the pilot.

In the lobby of the network you will see your competition, usually only two or three other actors. If there were an Olympic competition for actors, testing at the network would be it. It was in these lobbies that I witnessed the best-of-the-best actors preparing and focusing for their network read. It was also where I witnessed actors falling apart from nerves, from their ego whispering sweet nothings about money, and/or from self-sabotage generated by sudden, overwhelming insecurity.

It's exciting and scary, and no doubt tension and anticipation will fill the air, not just on the actor's part but from the executive producers as well, who are anxious that their material hits it home. The network has been very involved up to this point, with network development executives giving script notes to the writers and the network casting department collaborating with the casting office on actor recommendations.

Nonetheless, this is the first time network executives will be hearing the script out loud with actors saying the words. The bottom line is that the executive producers are still selling their pilot to the network brass.

The test is sometimes held in a screening room or space designed for these reads. Often it will have raised seats, as in a little movie theater, as well as a stage-like area with spotlights where you will stand. It can give off a bit of a theater vibe, so resist the impulse to become "theatrical." I encourage you to ask the casting director if you can have a peek at the room at the network before you walk in for your audition. This can alleviate the fear of the unknown, as discussed earlier. It's also a great idea to see where your light is and where the reader will be sitting, to make sure you have a chair if you need one, and to check out the size, shape, and acoustics of the room.

There might be as many as twenty or more people in this room; they will have added the Network President of Entertainment, the Head of Network Casting, the VPs of Drama or Comedy Development for the network, plus all the studio executives, your executive producers, the director, and the casting directors. This can be an intimidating room to walk into, to say the least, but you must enter it with confidence. First impressions are everything here. A lot of money will be spent on this project, and they want to make sure that you are confident, consistent, professional, and stable. They can tell all of those things just by the way you enter the room.

When you walk in, make sure you say hi and scan all the faces as if you were entering your living room and greeting guests. That's how comfortable and confident I want you to be. Take control of where you want the chair to be, thereby making it your space, not theirs. Remind yourself that this is for television and let the reader be your barometer for tone and volume. Next, take your five seconds to touch base with *place, relationship, intention,* and *pre-beat;* then look at the reader … and go.

The network executives have the final say as to which actor gets the part. Your executive producers and the studio executives have already signed off on you by bringing you here. They have brought the network a few choices, and hopefully someone will be cast. But it happens more often than you realize that no one is chosen, and the casting director has to go back to the drawing board.

Testing at the network is where I've observed actors finding the deep mental focus of an athlete, retreating into their bubble and tuning out all distractions. Images of the ice skater before competing in the Olympics, the gymnast on the balance beam, and the pitcher on the mound have flashed through my mind as I've witnessed the actor-athlete in action. This has held true whether actors have been testing for a comedy or drama.

Having the mental focus of an athlete will serve you well in this high-stress "actor Olympics" game. You have already scored big time by testing for the network. This is your opportunity to show your work to network executives who will now know who you are and will keep you in mind for other projects. It's a win-win situation.

11.2 THE CHEMISTRY READ

It is not uncommon at the network test for you to read with the star of the pilot or series who has already been cast. Or, you may have an individual read first with the casting director and then be "mixed and matched" with other actors for other parts. The goal here is to see if you have any chemistry with another actor, so by all means connect, and don't worry that it may be very different from all those past reads with the casting director. You now have another actor to play off, so go for it.

In this circumstance, the other actor will typically be standing to the side of you, a different configuration from when the casting director sat in a chair in front of you. When in this situation, actors often tend to upstage each other. So be mindful of this and turn to face the other actor, maybe cheating out just a little. Remember that what the network executives want to see is chemistry between you two.

Since this is possibly the first time you will have ever met the other actor, recalling the *relationship* you already established when you were reading previously with the casting director will be very helpful.

If there is hugging or kissing involved in the scene, I encourage you to make physical contact with the other actor, as this is one of the reasons you were given this scene to read in the first place. The viewers want to see if there are any sparks. If it looks like you are afraid to touch each other, it will scream *no chemistry between these two!*

Indulge me a moment with this cautionary tale from witnessing many chemistry reads that required kissing: Stage kissing only, please. No tongues.

11.3 The Screen Test

Screen tests are usually reserved for film, not television. Nonetheless, I have held screen tests a few times during my casting career, mainly when we were casting actors to portray real-life, often well-known people and needed the look and essence of the person to be a perfect match.

Similar to testing at the network, a screen test will concentrate on a handful of actors for the lead part. Your representatives will still need to negotiate a test option deal to set terms and your salary. Instead of auditioning "live" for the network executives, the executive producers will rent a studio in which to film your scenes. They will get you into full costume as well as hair and makeup and will probably hire professional actors to read opposite you. It is imperative that you be off-book for a screen test. It will be filmed as if it is a real shoot. The network will not view the screen test until after your deal is closed.

I held screen tests when I was casting the NBC miniseries *Liz: The Elizabeth Taylor Story,* produced by Lester Persky. We had about five different actresses get into full "Liz" hair and makeup, since the actress who played Elizabeth Taylor had to resemble her as closely as possible. We ended up casting the lovely Sherilyn Fenn as Liz. I remember reading in some magazine that of all the actresses who have played Elizabeth Taylor, Sherilyn Fenn was considered to look the most like her.

We also had screen tests when I was casting the CBS movie-of-the-week *Lucy & Desi: Before the Laughter,* produced by Larry Thompson. Larry and I held open calls in Los Angeles and Miami looking for the perfect Lucy and Desi, and I must say, it was one of the more interesting casting experiences I have ever had. I got hundreds if not thousands of pictures and resumes and phone calls from actors and actresses around the world, hoping to be our Lucy or Desi. The fact that these two people were so loved and recognizable put pressure on us to get the casting right.

* * * * * * * * * * * * * * * *

Before Larry Thompson and I went off to do our open calls, I held a few casting sessions for him for the part of Lucy. I already had a few actresses in mind and had also gotten submissions from various agents and managers I worked with and trusted. I wanted Larry to have a sense of who might be out there who could not only pull off looking like Lucy but who was also a professional actress.

One of the very first actresses who popped into my head to play Lucille Ball was Frances Fisher (Titanic, Resurrection). *Full disclosure, Frances and I are friends from our high school years in Orange, Texas. I watched Frances go from performing at the local community theater to her soap opera days when we were both in New York. When CBS transferred me from Director of Casting East Coast CBS to Director of Movies and Miniseries CBS Los Angeles, Frances and I got back in touch.*

When I know actors well, it sometimes colors my view—are they actually right for the role, or do I just like them as people? But with Frances's red hair, coupled with the fact that I knew she was a good actress with a facility for both comedy and drama, I had a feeling she might be "The One."

I brought Frances in to audition during that first casting session for Larry, and everyone really liked her. Then Larry and I trooped off on our traveling Lucy & Desi *sideshow, drumming up publicity as we went.*

By the time we got back to Los Angeles, it was clear to me that unknown, untrained actors could not carry the demanding parts of Lucy and Desi. It was a romantic idea to believe we could "discover" someone, and maybe we found a look-alike or two along the way. But there was no way that Lisa Freiberger, VP of Casting for CBS and my former boss, would let us cast a non-actor over a professional actor. Larry and I didn't want that either.

I brought Frances back in to audition a few more times and gathered as many existing film clips on her as possible, but everyone agreed that doing a full-blown screen test for the actors who would play Lucy and Desi was the only way anyone could make a decision.

I often tell the actors in my audition workshops that I have never seen an actress who better understood the difference in auditioning for the camera versus actually filming on the set than Frances Fisher. When Frances was auditioning for the part of

Lucille Ball, she knew that several people in the room watching were sitting a bit of a distance from her. She was also savvy that we were using a video camera that had a built-in microphone. Frances knew she had to be heard, so she projected her voice with just enough energy to be picked up by the microphone in the camera and spoke loudly enough so the producers could easily hear her.

When I showed up for the screen tests after all the actresses had gotten into full hair, makeup, and costume, I heard an actress from across the room filming her scenes. Then the room was cleared and it was Frances's turn. A boom hovered nearby to pick up her voice, the film camera was set close to her face, and the actor reading the part of Desi was almost nose to nose with her. When she began the scene, you could barely hear her. She was performing the same scene she had read multiple times in the various audition rooms, yet her energy and volume were completely adjusted to the circumstances. Frances understood how little volume she'd need to be heard and so delivered a conversational, authentic performance for the medium she was dealing with. This was an actress who understood film acting versus film auditioning. Frances was a brilliant Lucy.

11.4 The Hold

Once you sign your contract, you are in "first position" to this pilot or series, meaning that if you audition for another project and they want to test you, you will have to be in "second position" to that second project. Your representatives negotiate a finite time period you can be held after your audition at the network. The business affairs lawyers at the studio who negotiated with your reps will try to get a ten-business-day hold on you before they have to tell you if you booked the part or else release you from your test option deal.

Let's say your test at the network is on a Monday. Then, according to what the studio lawyers are asking, you would be held ten business days from Monday before they have to let you know if you are cast or not. Technically that is twelve days. In the middle of pilot season, when audition activity tends to be at its highest, it can be very frustrating for actors and their representatives if an actor has to sit around for twelve days not auditioning ... and then in the end not get cast in the project.

Rest assured, your representatives will try their best to whittle down the hold time. But what I really need you to understand is that the hold time is not in existence just to punish actors. So much of casting is finding chemistry among an entire cast, and that is a very hard thing to come up with. "Lightning in a bottle" is the term frequently used in assembling an ensemble cast of actors.

Even if the casting director has the good fortune to find an actor the network and everyone else loves for one of the leads in a pilot, it's possible the studio won't "pull the trigger" to pick up that actor's test deal until they make sure they can find an actress to play opposite him as his love interest. They might need the actors to read together to see if there is chemistry between them. That, in a nutshell, is the reason on the studio's side for trying to get as long a hold as possible. It's all about giving the casting director time to scramble to find the other actor who will have that "magic something" with you. On your representatives' side, they will try to find other projects willing to let you audition in second position. But not all casting directors like to bring in an actor to audition who is in second position. If their producers fall in love with an actor who ultimately isn't available ... well, you get the picture.

11.5 It's Their Option, Not Yours

2. PILOT OPTION DATE:

Studio shall have the exclusive option to employ Artist on a pay-or-play basis (pursuant to Paragraph 2 of the Standard Terms and Conditions attached hereto) for the Pilot (the "Pilot Option"), which Pilot Option is exercisable only by written notice from Studio's Business Affairs Department not later than ten (10) business days after the aforesaid test.

I could tell many different stories here about actors signing this contract at the studio test and changing their minds afterward about wanting to do the project. What seems like an amazing opportunity at the time can change when the actor and creator/ writer start having conflicts, or when one actor finds out he's making less money than his fellow actors, or when after three years on the show the actor is held to the meager bumps in his salary each year.

Understand that the contract that you sign at your test for the studio executives can follow you for many years. The studio holds all the cards here, because it is indeed a signed contract. I can tell you that the actor rarely wins when he tries to get out of this signed contract. With ratings success, your representatives may try to go back in to renegotiate a better money deal for you after the first few years, but higher salary is all tied to high ratings.

As widely reported in the press, David Caruso famously decided he wanted to get out of his contract on the hit series *NYPD Blue* after the first blockbuster year unless he was paid considerably more money. After bruising negotiations, Steven Bochco ultimately let him out of his long-term contract, but consequences were imposed as to how long it would be before David could commit to doing a network series again. After a few short years, David went on to star in the highly-rated *CSI: Miami*. So, I guess you could say things worked out just fine for Mr. Caruso.

However, in another scenario, even though *Scrubs* was a success with the audience and critics, it always struggled in the ratings, bounced around time periods, and finally changed networks. Zach Braff, the star of the show, was successful in renegotiating a higher salary. But several of the actors on that show were held to the contract they signed at the studio test, with those meager bumps in salary, for a long period of time.

When the representatives of two series regulars on *CSI: Crime Scene Investigation,* George Eads and Jorja Fox, tried to renegotiate the actors' contracts for more money several years back, the CBS brass threatened to replace the performers. So renegotiating a signed contract is not necessarily a given.

The best example of a successful contract renegotiation took place on behalf of the entire cast of *Friends*. It was reported that all the actors started out making $15,000 an episode in the first year, and the studio and network were playing hardball about giving the actors much more than the relatively meager bumps in salary from the original contract they'd signed at the studio test. As *Friends* soared to number one in the ratings and remained there, the entire cast along with all their representatives banded together, and in year ten they were getting a whopping $1 million *per episode.*

After this astounding renegotiation, all the studios started digging in their heels about holding to the terms of the signed contracts at the studio test, vowing to never be held hostage to this kind of maneuvering ever again. It still of course happens that agents are successful in getting big raises for actors when a series is a blockbuster in the ratings. But in today's economy, studios have strongly made their point that they won't make it an easy path to renegotiate a signed contract.

However, Jim Parsons, the star of *The Big Bang Theory,* managed to go from getting $350,000 per episode to $1 million per episode after a contract dispute that pushed back production of the eighth season for a week. So as you can see, with enormous popularity and ratings success, renegotiation is plausible.

For the most part though, actors will plan their exit from a popular show around when their contract expires. Josh Charles' contract was expiring on *The Good Wife* when he told the creators of the show, Robert and Michelle King, that he didn't want to re-up. That gave them the opportunity to write an amazing exit for Josh's character, even though the fans of the show may not have been happy with the outcome.

THE AUDITION BIBLE CHECKLIST

Testing at the Network

- ✔ You will be going to the network that has bought the pilot or series for your "test."
- ✔ If there were an Olympic competition for actors, testing at the network would be it.
- ✔ The executive producers are nervous as well, anxious for their material to score.
- ✔ The room you will be auditioning in at the network is often a screening room with a "theater feel" to it. Resist becoming "theatrical" in your audition.
- ✔ Make sure you enter the network test with confidence, because first impressions are everything here.
- ✔ Remind yourself that this is television, and let the reader be your barometer for tone and volume.
- ✔ It is possible that you will be "mixed and matched" with other actors to see if there is chemistry between you.
- ✔ If filming a "screen test," be off-book and at performance level. Prepare for full wardrobe and make-up.
- ✔ Know that once you sign the contract, you are bound to its terms. It's their option, not yours.

CHAPTER 12

YOU BOOKED THE PART

* * * * * * * * * * * * * * * *

It's hard to beat a person who never gives up.
Babe Ruth

12.1 THE TABLE READ

So you booked the part! You made it through the minefield of the audition process, and the studio has picked up your test option deal! Don't go buy that car quite yet. You still have the *table read* to get through.

On the first workday of the pilot or series, there will be a table read of the entire script with all the actors who have been cast. This literally means the full cast, the director, all the producers, the casting department, and various crew members such as the script supervisor sit around a table and read the script out loud. The table read of a pilot also is attended by the same studio and network executives who approved your being cast in the part.

Please don't take the phrase *table read* literally. I have witnessed some inexperienced actresses show up in sweatpants and no makeup thinking they were rehearsing. Not so. All the heavy-duty decision-makers will be in this room, and they want to witness a hit TV show in the making. Everyone is hoping this show will be their "lightning in a bottle," and this is the first glimpse into that magic.

You will need to be at performance level at the table read. Dress for the part just as you did in all of your auditions. Ladies, wear makeup. Be camera ready even though there will not be a camera in the room. The executives will be visualizing how you will look on TV screens across the world.

Unfortunately, there were a few times when I had to fire an actor after the table read. After all those individual auditions, only when the entire cast gets together in the same room do you discover if there is true chemistry in the air…or not. It may be unfair, but usually it's the actor who gets the blame when material isn't working, not the writer. And whatever that "certain something" is that is missing, the network executives will try to fix it by recasting one or more roles.

On-air series also have a table reading the first workday of each new episode. Actors who are series regulars on the show have been at this routine for a while, possibly years. They will show up relaxed, in sweats, possibly not having even looked at the new script. Guest and co-star actors on this one episode should not make the mistake of following suit. Guest actors should dress as they did in their audition and "bring it" to the table read. Don't give them an excuse to fire you.

12.2 The Studio and Network Run-Through

Half-hour comedies rehearse and shoot over a five-day period. If it is a situation comedy (sitcom), it is considered a *multicamera* show using four different cameras and usually shoots on a soundstage in front of an audience. A half-hour *single camera* show is just that; it uses one camera, usually shoots on location, and is not shot in front of an audience. An hour drama or dramedy shoots over an eight-day period and quite possibly could be filming at a location out of Los Angeles or New York.

Sitcoms are frequently shot on a studio lot in Los Angeles and are unique in that the studio and network executives like to come and watch a *run-through* to see how the show is shaping up so they can then give their notes. This usually happens on day two of the five-day shoot. The executives, producers, and the casting directors will follow along, walking from set to set on the soundstage to watch the run-through of the whole show. If an actor has never experienced this ritual, it can be a little disconcerting.

The actors are usually sent home for the day after the run-through and the executives huddle with the producers to give their notes on the script and the cast. As a casting director, I would always hold my breath, peeking over at the circle to try to read body language to see if they were discussing any actors. I dreaded that crooked finger aimed at me and the words "Holly, can you come join us?" Alternatively, I'd sigh with relief when I got a thumbs-up and was told I could leave.

The problem for the actor here is that there can be lots of cooks in the kitchen. The director of the episode might have a different take from the producers, who could have a different take from the executives. The best advice I can give actors who are cast in a sitcom is to be open to new direction and expect script changes constantly. Rewriting jokes happens even during the actual taping of the show, in front of the studio audience. If a joke doesn't elicit laughter from the audience, the writers will put their heads together and come up with new material on the spot. The actor is given a few minutes to learn the new lines, and then ... *show time!*

Leave your ego in your dressing room for the studio and network run-through. Be a team player, there for the good of the show, quick on your memorization skills, and able to switch direction on a dime. That is the nature of the sitcom beast.

* * * * * * * * * * * * * * * * * *

An actor in one of my classes told me he was once cast as a guest in a sitcom and felt things were going well. He got to tape night and the audience was in the house. The producers came up to him and said, "What you have been doing is great. But can you now make him gay?" Talk about a quick adjustment.

12.3 THE PICKUP

4. SERIES OPTION(S):

Provided Studio has exercised the Pilot Option, Studio shall have exclusive, successive, dependent annual options for Six (6) Series years if a fall season start (or Six and one-half (6-1/2) Series years if a mid-season start) to engage Artist's services in the Series.

First Series Year option is exercisable only by written notice to Artist given on or before June 30, 20XX. Studio shall have the option to extend its First Series Year option to December 31, 20XX by written notice to Artist on or before June 30, 20XX, followed by a payment in the amount of $XX,000 within ten (10) business days of Studio's notice of its exercise of such option.

Okay! You have gotten through the filming of the pilot! I wish I could tell you it was safe to buy that car now. But don't do it yet. Even if you have booked and shot the pilot, it doesn't necessarily mean your option will be picked up for the series.

After the pilot is shot and edited, the network will screen it for *test audiences.* The audience will be outfitted with clickers to respond to various questions and feelings about the actors. This is one tool used by the networks to judge whether a pilot has the potential to score with a wider audience and might be picked up for series, and it can also help determine whether an actor is kept on for the series or replaced.

I learned as a Network Executive for CBS during the grueling process of trying to decide if a pilot should be picked up, that the decision depends on a number of complex factors. Executives rely on a gut reaction, test audiences, and the clout of the executive producer (the creator of the show). If Shonda Rhimes, creator and executive producer of *Grey's Anatomy* and *Scandal,* shoots a new pilot, you can bet that her track record of great shows gives her a much better chance of her pilot making it to series.

Witness when ABC declared Thursdays "Shonda Rhimes Night" by scheduling her new show *How to Get Away with Murder* after *Grey's Anatomy* and *Scandal*. She was handed the "keys to the kingdom," a reward for producing blockbuster hits.

If the network decides they want to pick up your option for series, I might now say go ahead and buy that car. But remember that each year the studio has the right to exercise your option ... *or not* for the next six or seven years of the series.

12.4 The Upfronts

In the television industry, an *upfront* is an event hosted by television network executives that's attended by the press and advertisers. Its main purpose is to allow marketers to buy television airtime "up front," or several months before the television season begins.

The upfronts occur in New York City during the third week of May, when the networks announce their fall primetime schedules, including new on-air series. New series stars are trotted out in a dog-and-pony show, and clips are shown of the new series at large venues such as Madison Square Garden, Lincoln Center, or Radio City Music Hall.

Like the swallows coming back to Capistrano, the third week of May is when television touts its new season with a lot of hype to create buzz and attract advertisers.

With cable television stations like HBO and Showtime and online venues like Netflix and Amazon, which don't rely on advertisers, it is fascinating to see how the landscape of television (and what future role advertisers will play) is transforming, spiraling, and transporting us to parts unknown. It's very exciting to witness.

12.5 The Changing Landscape

The annual ritual called *pilot season* may end up being obsolete in the not too distant future. The landscape of television, especially "appointment TV," has been turned upside down. When I first started casting in the early 1980s, there were only three networks: ABC, CBS, and NBC. I remember when I cast one of the first pilots ever produced for Fox, I had a very difficult time getting agents to work on the project because it was an AFTRA contract and no one thought Fox would ever last.

With the explosion of cable, Netflix, recording devices, and the option of hundreds of channels, it's the Wild, Wild West out there. And the business of television as usual is no more.

I don't believe that even with the changing landscape of television that the audition process actors have to go through to book a job will change that drastically in the years to come. Unless an actor is already known to the producers of the project, has a demo reel that can sell him, or can book a role utilizing their on-camera audition, they will still have to troop into the audition room for the "powers that be."

However, actors now have more control over producing and acting in their own projects than ever before. Now anyone can have a fantastic idea, aim a camera, write her own webisode, post it on YouTube, and soon have thousands of followers ... and possibly a big fat money deal along the way. "New media" is changing and moving so fast, who can predict how that term will morph day to day?

Having started casting during the dinosaur age when there were only three networks, I can safely say that there has never been a better, more thrilling time to be an actor. Actors now have a plethora of opportunities before them and are able to generate their own work.

By tapping into your desires, by allowing your imagination to soar, and by being in tune with your thoughts, you will be amazed at what you will be able to manifest.

Dream it, think it, create it.

THE AUDITION BIBLE CHECKLIST

You Booked the Part

- ✔ Be at performance level at the table read, since studio and network executives will be attending and will expect it.

- ✔ During the studio and network run-through, stay open to direction and change, be a team player, get your ego out of the way, and be able to switch gears on a dime.

- ✔ Even if you have booked and shot the pilot, it doesn't necessarily mean your option will be picked up for the series.

- ✔ If your option is picked up for series, you are under contract for possibly six or seven years. And it is the option of the studio to renew your option each year ... *or not!*

- ✔ The upfronts happen the third week of May in New York City and are when the networks announce their new fall TV season with fanfare to the press and advertisers. Advertisers can buy "up front" advertising time before the series airs.

- ✔ *The times, they are a-changin'.*

Glossary

Agent – A representative who procures employment for actors and is licensed to do so by SAG-AFTRA, the actors union. The agent negotiates contracts on behalf of the actor and is paid 10 percent of the actor's earnings on each booked job.

Bump – The percentage that one's salary is increased each year on a television series.

Breakdown – A casting notice generated by the casting director of a show and released to talent agents and managers, containing short descriptions of each character as well as a brief synopsis of the plot and storyline.

Business Affairs – Lawyers who work for a studio, network, or production company and negotiate employment contracts with an actor's agent or representatives.

Callback – The invitation to come read again, this time usually for the director, producers, and writers, after an initial audition with the casting director.

Casting Director – A person or company hired by a studio, network, or production company to hold actor auditions for all the speaking roles in the script. The casting director not only negotiates contracts but is the liaison between the actors and their agents/managers and the producers, network, and studio.

Chemistry Read – The opportunity to read with the star or other actors being considered for roles in the pilot or series, in order to see if there is a spark or magic between two actors.

Demo Reel – Short clips or scenes of an actor's previous work edited together to showcase the performer's talent. A demo reel should be between two and five minutes long and contain the actor's best and strongest work.

Director – The person who directs the making of the show, visualizing how to shoot the script as well as guiding the crew and actors to fulfill that vision.

Executive Producer – Individual who adds their influence and business skills to helping the project get cast, financed and produced but does not usually take the daily responsibility. In television, it will also be the writer/creator of the show.

IMDb – Internet Movie Database, an online source of information related to films and TV that posts credits for actors, crew, and filmmakers, along with plot summaries.

Manager – An individual or company guiding the professional career of actors, offering advice and counsel on professional decisions and long-term plans. Managers are not required to be licensed by the actors union, SAG-AFTRA, and therefore are limited in their ability to personally negotiate contracts. The percentage paid to a manager varies from 10 percent to 20 percent of each booked job.

Mix and Match – An audition process during the final stages of casting a show, when actors may be asked to read with different partners to see if there is any chemistry between them and also how they look together. Playing off the other actor is key at this stage, quite different from reading with the casting director or a reader.

Open Call – A large-scale audition open to all professional or nonprofessional actors, sometimes referred to as a "cattle call."

Pilot – The first episode of a proposed new series for network television, after which network executives decide whether to order additional episodes, and if so to give it a time slot on the schedule.

Pre-Read – An audition for the casting director only, to determine if an actor will be seen by the producers and director for a callback.

Quotes – The amount of money and other contractual deal points an actor made on previous jobs.

Show Runner – The person who has the creative and managerial control over all the day-to-day aspects of running a television production; also serves as a producer on the show

Sides – Specific scenes in a script given to an actor to prepare for an audition.

Slate – An actor's identification before a taped audition, made by standing on a marked spot and stating his or her name to the camera.

Table Read – The organized reading of a script around a table by the actors with speaking parts, typically attended by the writers, director, producers, casting director, and studio and network executives.

Test Audience – A group of non-industry people invited to attend a preview screening of a television pilot or film. Producers gauge their reaction to the storyline and the characters by asking them to provide feedback.

Test Option Deal – Also know as a TOD, the contract an actor must sign before testing for a series-regular role on television. The actor's representatives negotiate the contract with someone in business affairs representing the studio. Details such as the actor's salary for the pilot and/or series, length of time commitment (often a six or seven year time period), and bumps in salary are covered in the TOD. The studio has the sole option to pick up the actor's services for both the pilot and, if ordered, the series, or else to release that actor entirely.

Testing at the Network – The final audition an actor has when competing for a series-regular role on television. The actor will have already signed a contract (test option deal) before being allowed to read at the network. The network executives will make the final determination as to whether the actor is cast in the part or not.

Tone – The overall form of a show, set by the writer; in television this translates into whether the show is a comedy, drama, or dramedy.

Upfronts – An Industry event, hosted by television network executives and attended by the press and advertisers, to encourage marketers to buy television airtime "up front," or several months before the television season begins. The upfronts take place in New York City during the third week of May, when the networks announce their fall primetime schedules, and are held at large venues such as Madison Square Garden, Lincoln Center, or Radio City Music Hall.

Work Session – Before the studio or network test, the chance for an actor to work through the audition material with the director and producers. This usually includes some initial blocking and direction, so that the actor will feel more prepared and confident.

RESOURCES FOR ACTORS

ONLINE SERVICES

Actors Access: www.actorsaccess.com

Backstage: www.backstage.com

Breakdown Services: www.breakdownexpress.com

CastingAbout: www.castingabout.com

Create Your Reel: www.createyourreel.com

iActing Studios: www.iActingstudios.com

IMDb: www.imdb.com

LA Casting: www.lacasting.com

Now Casting: www.nowcasting.com

BOOKSTORES

The Drama Book Shop: www.dramabookshop.com

Samuel French Bookshop: www.samuelfrench.com/bookstore

AGENT AND CASTING DIRECTOR GUIDES

The Actor's Guide to Agents
by Samuel French

Call Sheet
by Backstage

C/D Directory: The Professionals Casting Directory
by Breakdown Services

RECOMMENDED BOOKS

Acting Is Everything: An Actor's Guidebook for a Successful Career in Los Angeles
by Judy Kerr

Acting with Impact: Power Tools to Ignite the Actor's Performance
by Kimberly Jentzen

An Agent Tells All
by Tony Martinez

The Artist's Way: A Spiritual Path to Higher Creativity
by Julia Cameron

Audition
by Michael Shurtleff

The Four Agreements: A Practical Guide to Personal Freedom
by Don Miguel Ruiz

How to Be a Working Actor: The Insider's Guide to Finding Jobs in Theatre, Film, and Television
by Mari Lyn Henry and Lynne Rogers

How to Get Arrested: A Motivational Story for Actors Breaking into Hollywood
by Michael J. Wallach

The Mental ABC's of Pitching: A Handbook for Performance Enhancement
by H. A. Dorfman

On the Set: The Hidden Rules of Movie Making Etiquette
by Paul J. Salamoff

The Power of Intention
by Dr. Wayne W. Dyer

The Power of Now: A Guide to Spiritual Enlightenment
by Eckhart Tolle

Riding the Alligator: Strategies for a Career in Screenplay Writing (and not getting eaten)
by Pen Densham

The 7 Habits of Highly Effective People: Powerful Lessons in Personal Change
by Stephen R. Covey

The Seven Spiritual Laws of Success: A Practical Guide to the Fulfillment of Your Dreams
by Deepak Chopra

The Sitcom Career Book: A Guide to Louder, Faster, Funnier
by Mary Lou Belli and Phil Ramuno

Strategic Acceleration: Succeed at the Speed of Life
by Tony Jeary

The Success Principles: How to Get from Where You Are to Where You Want to Be
By Jack Canfield

The War of Art: Break Through the Blocks and Win Your Inner Creative Battles
By Steven Pressfield

Holly Powell began her casting career in New York casting off-Broadway theater. Soon hired as Director of Casting East Coast for CBS, she then transferred to Los Angeles to take over as their Director of Casting Movies and Miniseries.

Holly next partnered with Randy Stone, forming Stone Powell Casting. They won an Emmy Award for "Outstanding Achievement in Casting for a Miniseries or a Special" for casting *The Incident* starring Walter Matthau. She also won the Casting Society of America's Artios Award as well as receiving multiple CSA nominations over the years.

Bob Greenblatt and David Janollari hired Holly to be their Senior VP of Talent and Casting for The Greenblatt Janollari Studio, where she worked on multiple projects including *Six Feet Under* by Alan Ball. She later partnered with Liz Melcher forming Powell Melcher Casting where they cast cult favorites *The Twilight Zone* and *The 4400,* among many other projects.

In 2006 she made the transition from casting to teaching forming Holly Powell Studios (www.hollypowellstudios.com) in Los Angeles, an audition studio for actors, and quickly won The Backstage Readers' Choice Award for Favorite Audition Technique Teacher two years in a row. She has taught her audition workshops at colleges, universities, drama schools, and at organizations across the country.

Holly lives in Studio City, California with her husband, Chris Wright, who is a talent manager at Wright Entertainment. Their son, Ryan Wright, is currently attending Reed College in Portland, Oregon.